FAT
GIRL
SLIM

FAT GIRL SLIM

RUTH WATSON

Photography by Georgia Glynn Smith

Quadrille

FOR DARLING, THROUGH FAT AND THIN

First published in 2003 by
Quadrille Publishing Limited,
Alhambra House,
27-31 Charing Cross Road,
London WC2H 0LS

Reprinted in 2004
10 9 8 7 6 5 4 3 2

Text © Ruth Watson 2003
Photography © Georgia Glynn Smith 2003
Design & layout © Quadrille Publishing Ltd 2003

Editorial Director: **Jane O'Shea**
Art Director: **Helen Lewis**
Editor & Project Manager: **Lewis Esson**
Design Assistant: **Ros Holder**
Photography: **Georgia Glynn Smith**
Production: **Jane Rogers**

Cataloguing in Publication Data: a catalogue record for this book is available from the British Library

ISBN 1 84400 046 X

Printed and bound in China

ACKNOWLEDGEMENTS

The greatest thanks to Fiona Pow for coming up with a brilliant title (and Norman Cook for being so cool about it). Thank you to Murray Arbeid, Freddy Fox, Rhona O' Brien and Alison Cathie for providing the conduit of friendship that has resulted in this book. (It's not what you know...) I am immensely grateful to Jane O' Shea, Helen Lewis and Lewis Esson for their dogged but diplomatic professionalism, and to James Perry for helping me cook the food that Georgia Glynn Smith (and Daisy) photographed with such sparky panache. Thank you to Nigel Slater for much, and everyone at the Crown and Castle for coping so well with my frequent absences. And, lots of love to Jessie and Jack.

Contents

FAT GIRL Whom?

Yesterday I called on willpower, that uncertain ally, to stop me eating something. As usual, it didn't work – it seldom does. Fortunately the local baker had burnt that day's delivery of gorgeous, oil-pooled, rosemary and sea salt focaccia, so I was saved – at least temporarily.

I haven't always been fat. For the first 21 years of my life I was actually quite slim – lithe enough to model jeans at one stage. It was only when I got married that I started putting on weight. Nevertheless, I hold my mother entirely to account for my fixation with food – and not simply because it's the fashion nowadays to blame one's parents for every ill, imagined or otherwise. Utterly atypical for an English woman of the Fifties – especially one with a paltry income – my mother valued good food above everything else. Well, everything except for Start-rite shoes, properly fitted, of course. (I don't like to think how often my feet went into the X-ray machine in Clarks shoe shop: adults and children alike regarded it as a toy, not a potentially dangerous piece of medical equipment.) The upshot was we had neither holidays, central heating nor a car, but we did have the first wild salmon of the season, white peaches in August and a huge sirloin of roast beef, complete with fillet, every Sunday. There were even a few cases of wine in the cellar, hugger-mugger with a big pile of Coalite (she was a snob about good fuel, too). Even more oddly, in an era when few working-class households had any refrigeration at all, she managed to scrape together enough money to buy an enormous American fridge that stood, cream and curvy, in the corner of the breakfast room.

The reason I wasn't fat when I was young is probably because I was always out playing – in the street, on top of the defunct air-raid shelters or down by the brook. Computer games hadn't been invented and if child molesters existed, they weren't in Finchley. Daily sports activities, too, were still an integral part of the school curriculum. It also helped that we ate not just lavishly, but properly. I don't know whether my mother consciously applied intellect to our diet, or whether she simply bought what she fancied cooking (and the seasons provided) but we ate what would now be recognised as a perfectly balanced diet. While I try very hard to forget our lurid, orange-painted breakfast room, I can still see the lilac Formica table (so harmonious with the walls), permanently heaped with fruit. My mother was incapable of buying a mere half-dozen nectarines or a punnet of strawberries, when she could purchase a whole tray: muscat grapes were bought in multiple bunches, tangerines by the net, and even melons arrived home mob-handed. Most meals started with proper soup of some sort or another and the main course was always accompanied by a large quantity of fresh vegetables. Even more

miraculously, they were not overcooked, my mother being a big fan of Elizabeth David, as well as Tante Marie and Constance Spry. (But not Fanny Craddock, whom she detested. "How can she possibly make pastry wearing those rings?" was a frequent jibe, along with a myriad aspersions on Mrs Craddock's over-plucked eyebrows, inappropriate clothing and lack of hygiene: "It's quite disgusting – she never washes her hands".)

Of course, I also ate sweets but they were strictly a once-a-week affair, bought with my hard-earned pocket money. So, unless I could find an Everton Mint lurking in the bottom of my father's capacious cardigan pocket, the only rubbish I ate was on Saturday morning. (Actually, that's libellous – never could Brown Cow, that divine confection of soft vanilla ice cream drowned in Coca-Cola, be described as rubbish.)

My trips to the sweet shop owned by Mr White (who I always thought was the R. White of lemonade fame) were usually hijacked by my mother's own shopping demands. Naturally, I was not averse to popping into Cullen's for a pound of broken biscuits or, on high days and holidays, chocolate Viennas, but I wasn't quite so keen on buying the fish. The best errand by far was when I had to go to Pauline's to get the bread. Usually our order was for a large farmhouse or Danish but, occasionally – rare joy of joys – I was allowed to buy a more expensive cottage loaf. Unlike modern supermarkets, where aerosols not hot ovens supply the wonderful smell of baking, Pauline's bread was genuinely made on the premises – and, boy, did it taste like it. It was a rare occasion when I managed to bring a loaf home, completely unbroached. Even more shamefully, I didn't tear into the warm, fragrant bread in an orderly fashion but ripped out the soft-hearted crumb, leaving the crust to conceal the ravages. (Nowadays I prefer the crust, but that's maturity for you.)

In many ways I am thankful for the emphasis placed on good food while I was growing up. And, if I hadn't loved food and been reasonably knowledgeable about it, my husband and I wouldn't have bought Hintlesham Hall in 1983, nor would we have gone on to buy another famous hostelry, the Fox and Goose Inn at Fressingfield. Now we are the proprietors of the Crown and Castle, an 18-bedroom hotel in Orford, on the Suffolk coast just down from Aldeburgh. (Spot the blatant plug.)

But sometimes I rather resent the stranglehold food has on me and the way it has become both my life and livelihood. There's seldom a day when I am not doing something that involves food. Much of the week I am talking about recipes and menus with my chefs and trying out new dishes for the Trinity, the bistro which is at the hub of our hotel. I fantasise about food during the day and dream about it at night. I go to the local farmers' market and spend long hours seeking out local food producers. I grow many of my own vegetables, herbs and soft fruit. I keep empty food packets to remind me of what was good and who made it. I buy magazines (British and foreign), as well as the weekend newspapers, purely on the worth of their food and restaurant columns. I tear out recipes and articles about food and file every bit of bumf about food shops and mail order companies. I order food on-line and have bookmarks for more food-related web sites than anything else. I dream about food and plan holidays around it, selecting countries on the strength of their restaurants, rather than the climate or number of art galleries. In a nutshell (preferably salted pistachio), I adore food.

I also worry about food and feel guilty about what I've eaten and what I am planning to eat. None of this would matter if I was naturally lean, but the sad truth is that food loves me every bit as much as I love it. It clambers up my shoulders and turns into folds at the back of my neck; it clings round my belly and hips in bulging hillocks; it dimples my elbows and knees; it swells my bosom into a bulbous bolster; it even renders my feet and ankles elephantine. Coming to an agreement with food that allows me the pleasure without the porcine penalty has been the bane of my life.

But a year ago – and after half a lifetime of being fat – I managed to lose over 4 stone. The remarkable thing is that I didn't stop cooking or eating. And, with only the odd wobble, I found the whole experience much less harrowing than I had anticipated.

I would never pretend that I was now slim (despite the title of my book), merely unremarkable – and that suits me very well. Fat people are such easy targets. Accompanying the misery of not being able to paint one's own toe nails or wear a pair of one-size tights is the knowledge that obesity also carries the stigma of feckless, lazy, self-indulgence. The fact that there are plenty of rake-thin teenagers who nosh an unremitting diet of chicken nuggets and pizza, and spend endless days mouldering in bed, should suggest that an over-consumption of calories and a paucity of physical exercise is not just the preserve of fat people: everyone knows someone who eats like a horse, exercises like a snail, but doesn't put on a pound.

According to the latest research from Addenbrooke's Hospital in Cambridge, 30–40% of the susceptibility to becoming fat could be explained by genetic factors. Dr Finer, an obesity expert there, is quick to add that extra flab cannot be blamed solely on one's genetic make-up but that there may be underlying mechanisms that make it harder to keep weight under control. Patently, this is desperately unfair on those of us who don't possess a handy little fat-burning gene – but maybe we have another gene that fends off liver cancer or schizophrenia: it's the luck of the draw.

The only problem is that while a cancer victim deservedly attracts sympathy, being fat engenders nothing but derision. I still remember a particular incident with chagrin. Driving towards traffic lights that were in my favour, a chap stepped off the pavement straight in front of me. His reaction to my startled warning toot was a spew of invective. No prizes for guessing it included the words 'fat' and 'cow'. While this was by no means a core reason for my decision to knuckle down and lose weight (see page 20) occasions like this do help contribute to the feeling of self-loathing that so often accompanies being fat.

Nevertheless, I really am not prepared to accept that the concept of guilt or innocence should be attached either to food itself or anyone who enjoys eating it. Unfortunately, it's a notion that crops up all the time in the context of dieting. How often do you hear or read that food is 'naughty' or 'sinful' or that the dieter has been 'really good' or 'so bad'. Intellectually, I just don't buy this nonsense; emotionally, it's hard to resist. Part of my campaign to continue eating well while losing weight is in defiance of the idea that food can somehow corrupt one's integrity. Too much food can certainly be to the detriment of one's health, but it should not be permitted to impinge negatively on one's psyche.

Reactions to my weight loss have been similarly tainted with an implied moral judgement. One very good friend has never mentioned it, something I find quite extraordinary and rather dispiriting as far as my relationship with her goes. Then there are people I haven't seen for a while who almost levitate with shocked pleasure at the change in my appearance. Others closer to me compliment me lavishly and frequently on my improved looks. Naturally, this is very pleasant to hear, but it's also oddly irritating. It's as if the new me is more worthy in some way than the old me. The fact that I am no less or more bad-tempered/sweet-natured, lazy/conscientious, kind/catty, generous/mean, stupid/intelligent, talented/useless now than when I was four stone heavier seems irrelevant.

There is also the problem that I have never been able to see myself as others do. I look at photos of myself when I was young and see a demonstrably good-looking girl. (No false modesty here: what's the point.) But that's absolutely not how I felt at the time. I realise this is not unique to me; most women regret not having realised quite how lovely youth is in itself, never mind a classic configuration. Nor have I ever been able to envisage just how gross I undoubtedly looked when at my fattest. It's partly to do with my belief that virtue should be embodied in one's soul and not one's looks: it's also partly to do with an innate scorn for people who are vain. I find such beings shallow, which is probably as stereotypical a standpoint as any levelled at fat people.

The really significant aspect of my weight loss is not my outward appearance but the way I feel inside – brisker mentally, more lighter-hearted and, yes, happier. And, health-wise, there has been a fantastic improvement. I no longer suffer aches or pains in my knees and hips, nor do I have indigestion, palpitations, night panics, incipient incontinence or sundry other mildly debilitating complaints. All those general practitioners who are constantly telling patients they need to diet should go further: "Sorry, missus, not one scrap of medical treatment until you've lost x stone." Whether the methods or the nutritional content of my diet are scientifically sound is really of little moment. None of us acts, eats or behaves flawlessly all the time, whether dieting or not. I certainly did not eat perfectly – some days I had far too little, some days far too much. Some days I was active, others (many others) I did precious little other than sit at my desk. The fact is that everything I did – rightly or wrongly – has resulted in my being substantially thinner.

It's no surprise that I have been bombarded with the same one question, "How did you do it?" While it's tempting to say that I just ate less, it wouldn't be true – and even if it were it wouldn't be the whole story.

But I understand why there's a burning need to know because, despite the countless slimming books on sale, few seem to be directed at intelligent people who like cooking and eating. The vast majority seem to fall into three categories. The first group believes that the key to a perfect figure is interminable exercise, the sort of manic jerking as espoused by Jane Fonda et al: eating is anathema. The second reduces food to little more than a collection of chemical compounds that have to be either eschewed, manipulated or ingested in certain combinations – and at the right time of day, of course. Only by following a strict set of rules will optimum nutritional value be obtained and, thus, a healthy body. The idea that food is more than the sum of its parts and that eating should be a joyful experience doesn't enter into it. Lastly, there are the slimming magazines that are only interested in telling their readers about the fat content of the latest lita-bite, whoppakrisp. Only if you think Mariah Carey is a fine soprano would you want to follow their advice.

And that's the main reason for writing this book – a book that doesn't just tolerate food but celebrates it, albeit in a somewhat circumscribed way. It's all about food as a subject that's innately exciting and quite wonderful to eat. Apart from being a food snob, I am also a restaurateur and a food writer. More importantly, I was – and still would and could be – a fat woman. Yet I have managed to lose a considerable amount of weight without resorting to drugs, staples, tucks or liposuction. Vitally, every word I have written about my diet is the undiluted truth, warts and all. It's certainly not a counsel of perfection as posited by some chopstick-thin journalist who has never had a weight problem in her life. This is about what a fat person did, for better or worse.

By now it should be obvious that if I can diet so can anyone. There are only two things that may possibly set me apart from anyone else intent on slimming, namely a few bob in the bank and the ability to cook. The latter doesn't matter. You can learn to cook (perhaps from this book?) but if you prefer not to, there's nothing to stop you eating unprocessed or raw food, or buying good food that someone else has cooked. Mail order companies, supermarkets and specialist food shops abound with ready-prepared meals and some of them are really quite good. As for money, I have no answer except to say that if you can afford cigarettes, booze, cars, designer clothes or holidays, you can afford to eat well – it's all a matter of priority. For me, paradise is not lying on a Caribbean beach but being served a bowl of tagliolini strewn with white truffle. I really hope you enjoy reading this book, using the recipes and losing weight. But even if you remain as fat as a Christmas goose, I'm still on your side. Because, despite everything, I still believe that beauty is to do with what's in your heart, not what's on your hips.

a few bits and pieces that will help you use this book

Quantities

It will say at the top of each recipe how many it feeds. Just bear in mind that although appetites vary, on the whole I veer towards the generous. Because much of this book is to do with solo eating there will be times when you won't want to use up a whole tin or packet of food. This doesn't matter a fig if it's something like rice cakes (or figs) but you won't want to waste half a can of expensive piquillo peppers. Obvious though it may be, simply tip the remaining contents into a small non-reactive, sealable container and refrigerate it – and use before mould starts growing on the top.

The clip-on/clip-off concept

One of the special features of *Fat Girl Slim* is that it allows you and your partner to eat in harmony. To facilitate this I have devised a concept whereby **'more'** or **'less'** appendices at the end of (many) recipes will give hints on how to add or subtract extra protein, fat or carbohydrate. This should prevent the non-dieting partner feeling aggrieved: similarly the dieter (you) won't feel tempted or coerced into eating more than is wanted. The clip-on/clip-off concept works as well with flavours as it does with extra bulk. What could be easier than dividing a stir-fry in half and adding a handful of crabmeat to one bowl and some cooked chicken to the other? Well, spreading marmalade on toast – but you get my drift. Cooking for two disparate appetites does not have to be a stressful, difficult experience. It just requires a little forethought.

Peeling (and other details)

I have decided that if I am bored with too much detail in recipes then you may be too. So, I have ditched all those instructions to peel onions or warm dishes or preheat ovens. I am going to assume that you know the basics and only if a recipe calls for an onion to remain unpeeled or a cooked chicken breast to be pulled – rather than cut – into shreds will I tell you.

Chopping and cutting

Chopping instructions can be ambiguous. For example, a finely chopped leek is going to end up in rather larger pieces than a finely chopped clove of garlic or a chilli. Then there is the problem of grammar: 'chopped medium' is ghastly but 'chopped mediumly' sounds utterly stupid, however fond one is of adverbs. So here's what I mean.

Herbs *Finely chopped* means the herbs should have completely lost their discernible form without looking like a pile of green dandruff. When a herb is chopped too small it's the board that benefits (from all the aromatic oil embedded in it) not the recipe. *Roughly chopped* means the form of the leaf will still be recognisable, albeit hacked about. (If you come across an instruction to use only the leaves it's because the texture of the stalks may be too coarse for that particular recipe, but don't waste them – put them in the stock pot. Otherwise chop the whole lot up.)

finely chopped

roughly chopped

Vegetables Everything will depend on the original size of the vegetable, but as a rule of thumb *finely chopped* means the size of butcher's mince; *cut into small dice* means about the size of Dolly Mixtures (with thanks to Nigel Slater for an unsurpassed analogy); *chopped into small bite-sized chunks* or *cubes* or *cut into medium dice* means pieces about the size of a postage stamp (bearing in mind that if it refers to a red pepper we are talking 2D but in the case of a potato it will be 3D.) Finally, if it says *chopped into large bite-sized chunks* or *cubes* you should be thinking of chunks about the size of a toasted marshmallow.

small bite-sized chunks

large bite-sized chunks

small dice

finely chopped

Blanching Although you can blanch many foods, it's normally vegetables that require this preliminary service. All it means is bringing a very large volume of water to the boil, throwing in the veg for the time specified (e.g. garlic cloves 3–4 minutes; asparagus or French beans destined for a salad, 2–3 minutes; herbs 30 seconds) then immediately draining (and refreshing) them – see below. Strictly speaking, the par-boiling of potatoes before roasting them counts as blanching but the technique is mainly used in recipes where there is a paucity of liquid in the final cooking process or where the cooking time is very short or when the vegetable is destined for a salad.

Refreshing Often a recipe will call for something to be 'refreshed' straight after it has been blanched. This is nothing more than a quick dunk into ice-cold water which helps stops the cooking process and, in the case of green vegetables and herbs, fixes the colour.

Let down This has nothing to do with lowering trouser hems or how you felt when your parents didn't show up for the only sports day when you won a race. In culinary terms it is (normally) applied to a sauce that requires extra liquid in order to create a thinner consistency. Think of the difference between the thin custard used for Floating Islands and the thicker custard required for a traditional English trifle.

Warming plates I don't want to sound snotty but I am constantly amazed at how many people serve hot food on cold plates. It's like skiing in Jamaica – you just don't do it. Or not if you want to enjoy every scrap of your meal and not just the first few mouthfuls. Now most people have double ovens, it's the work of a few seconds to put plates and serving dishes in to warm, but if you forget (rather than can't be bothered) fill a sink with the hottest water possible and soak the plates for a few minutes, until they have warmed up.

Oven temperatures This is a colossally boring but important subject. In fact, I think I may go and make myself an espresso before I begin. Right, let's start with the difference between fan ovens and fan-assisted ovens. In the latter, the top and bottom elements provide the heat – the fan merely circulates it – and you have to wait for the elements to heat up, just as in a conventional oven. However, a 'proper' fan oven has an element that encircles the fan at the back of the oven and produces hot air right from the outset. This means food can be put in the oven straight away, which reduces the cooking time. Exceptions are dishes which require a fierce initial blast, such as Yorkshire pudding, scones, bread or puff pastry, or something that takes only a few minutes to cook. And, because the heat is transferred more efficiently to the food in both types of oven, lower temperatures can be used. I use the Good Housekeeping Institute's conversion chart which suggests a 20°C reduction. As the recipes in *Fat Girl Slim* have all been tested in a real fan oven, raise the heat by 20°C if you are using a conventional oven. But please don't regard this as an inviolable rule: ovens vary, whatever their heating methods, and you should always be prepared to lower or raise temperatures and extend or shorten cooking times, as necessary.

Amounts of oil and butter Fat is highly calorific, so when a recipe calls for a 'scrap of butter' or a 'drop of oil', I do mean the teeniest amount you can get away with – not a who-cares knob of butter or a happy-go-lucky slug of oil. Using a non-stick pan helps, as does swirling the hot fat round the pan to coat it, then throwing away the surplus before adding the food.

a witter about ingredients

Salt and pepper It sounds like a counsel of perfection, it sounds smug, it sounds expensive, it sounds too 'foodie' for words, but if you've never bothered about the quality of the salt and pepper you buy, it will come as something of a revelation if you use sea salt rather than table salt, and whole black peppercorns rather than ready-milled white pepper.

Sea salt has a more acute flavour than ordinary table salt and thus you don't need to use so much. It is also free of additives – table salt incorporates magnesium oxide to guarantee a smooth flow. More importantly, sea salt contains a variety of other natural minerals that give it a greater complexity of flavour. You can buy sea salt in many different forms from bright-white flakes (Maldon) to dirty-looking crystals (Guérande). Smart food shops also sell the fiercely expensive 'fleur de sel', which is regarded as the cream of the crop: I am not sure that the price is justified, but it's worth a fling now and again.

Pre-ground pepper is not bad the first time you open the jar, but from then on it's downhill all the way. Far better to have a mill filled with whole peppercorns and grind them to order. This way, all the volatile oils that give pepper its characteristic flavour are only released when and as you want them, rather than dissipating into thin air each time you open the jar. Black peppercorns are whole sun-dried berries and have a full, complex flavour. White peppercorns have had the skins removed and give a sharper, hotter taste. When I suggest seasoning a *Fat Girl Slim* recipe you can assume that it's sea salt and freshly ground black pepper I am hoping you will use.

Mussels (and clams) Dirty, barnacle-encrusted mussels are a much rarer occurrence than they used to be, mostly because so many mussels are farmed (i.e. rope-grown) nowadays. Even so, they still need a really thorough wash in cold water. The 'beards' with which the bivalves anchor themselves down must also be removed. This is the hairy-looking tuft that can be found wedged between the two shells: simply tear it out. You must also discard any mussels that remain open before cooking, although afterwards it is any closed mussels that need to be chucked away.

Greenland prawns I really would appreciate it – and so will you – if you use whole Greenland (or North Atlantic) prawns in the recipes that follow, not the ready-peeled ones that look like some kind of wet pink larvae. Prawns you have peeled yourself have a markedly better flavour and a firm, meaty texture. And, apart from gaining a superior product, the debris can be made into a free and fabulous shellfish stock. As a rough guide, 225g of whole prawns yields about 85g of meat.

Root ginger In just the same way that old carrots and parsnips are tougher and coarser-textured than young ones, so too is over-mature root ginger. It's not easy to determine the degree of maturity, but if you end up with a hairy, fibrous mass after grating a 'thumb' of ginger, discard it and use only the soft pulp.

Garlic Believe it or not, it matters if a clove of garlic is crushed or not before being chopped. The reason for this is quite simple: when crushed, the cell walls collapse and release an enzyme that magnifies the taste. For most cooked dishes, an intense flavour is exactly what is wanted – but not in a mild-mannered dish, where only a gentle hint of garlic is required. In this instance, chop the garlic but don't bash it first.

essential store cupboard items

Piquillo peppers Dutch peppers and their lack of flavour, not to mention the fag of having to grill them to remove the tough skin, is why I normally prefer to use tinned Spanish red peppers, preferably a variety called piquillo. These brilliant-red peppers are roasted over wood chippings (not in some industrial oven); the skins are removed by hand (rather than with a high-pressure hose); and the liquid they are packed in is olive oil (not brine). This means they are not cheap but they are good to eat – which is okay, in my book.

Marigold Swiss vegetable bouillon powder What a mouthful, in more senses than one. Unlike many other brands of stock powder, Marigold does not taste like a chemical by-product, nor does it sport a hideous tangerine scum. Most supermarkets stock it, which is just as well as it underpins much of my dietary cooking.

Thai fish sauce (nam pla) Fish sauce is as fundamental to Thai cooking as soy sauce is to Chinese. In itself the flavour borders on the irresistibly repellent, but blended with other core Thai ingredients, such as lemon grass and galangal, it supplies an inimitable, savoury punch. The strangely named Squid brand is my favourite (and is probably the best) although Blue Dragon seems to have colonised most of the supermarket shelves.

Dashi Part of the essential Japanese octet (the others being mirin, soy sauce, noodles, sake, tofu, Japanese rice and dried seaweed), dashi is a 'universal' stock that can be made from scratch with kombu (seaweed) and bonito (dried tuna) but which lazy tykes, like me, buy in powder form from supermarkets with an Asian section, or from specialist Japanese food shops. In an emergency, nick the little sachet from a packet of ramen (readily available) and use that instead.

Shiitake broth I find this dark brown, 'meaty' brew invaluable for adding instant but genuine flavour to Oriental dishes, especially noodles: with grated ginger and daikon (white radish or mooli) it also makes a great dip for (non-dietary) tempura. You can find it in Sainsbury's Special Selection and health food shops.

Instant miso soup A concoction of fermented soy beans, onions and seaweed (diluted with water), miso soup is sweet, earthy and fragrant. And before you contort your face into an expression of disgust, remember that whisky and beer are made from mashed-up grains that have been left to rot under controlled conditions. Sanchi Instant Miso Soup comes in little red boxes and can be found in the better supermarkets and leading health food shops.

Teriyaki marinade/sauce Chicken yakitori is as popular with Westerners as it is with the Japanese, who devote whole restaurants to serving only grilled gobbets of offal, meat and fish, marinated in sweetish, soy-based teriyaki sauce. Sanchi is a good organic brand and Blue Dragon the most ubiquitous, but to my mind the best and most authentic is made by Kikkoman.

Mirin This sweetish alcohol (about 13%) is used in Japanese cooking, especially for marinades, dipping sauces and teriyaki. It is often erroneously described as sweet sake, but is actually made from distilled spirit, rice and the same bacterial culture used in soy sauce.

Wasabi There are many misconceptions about Japanese food (the greatest being that it is entirely composed of raw fish – and slimy fish, at that) and one of them is that the chilli-hot green paste served with sashimi is Japanese horseradish – although it doesn't actually belong to the horseradish family. And the stuff that comes in tubes is often adulterated with ordinary mustard: the packet I am looking at now also contains sorbitol, emulsifier, turmeric and Brilliant Blue FCF – which sounds too much like a Korean football club for comfort. I should stick to the little tins of wasabi powder and make it into a paste yourself.

Nori I have some sympathy with food producers who try to market seaweed as a sea vegetable. I just find it slightly odd that while the Welsh tuck into laverbread (also seaweed) with gay abandon, the English cringe in horror at the notion. I put it down to the belief that all seaweed must be tough and slippery – it's that perennial textural problem – but nori is actually the thin, dry stuff you find wrapped round many types of sushi. I cut it into fine strips and strew it on soup, rice and noodles for an ambiguous, mossy flavour.

Hijiki Another seaweed, hijiki is one of my top ten favourite foods. The flavour is impossible to describe – partly because it is almost overwhelmed by the dashi, soy, mirin and sugar–flavoured stock it is so often cooked in. Looking a bit like shiny giant tea leaves,

I love the slightly chewy texture, fabulous ebony colour and the fact it goes so well with noodles, tofu and vegetables, such as carrots. You can buy hijiki in leading supermarkets and health food shops.

Tamari A wheat-free type of soy sauce, tamari is rich, dark and has a bit more poke than ordinary soy. It's also the answer to those who profess to have a wheat allergy (and, yes, you can detect a hint of scepticism).

Japanese soy sauce On the whole, I prefer Japanese soy sauce to Chinese, finding it smoother and with less of an acrid Marmite-kick at the end.

Furikake This Japanese seasoning combines black and white sesame seeds, granulated nori seaweed and red shiso leaves. Sprinkled over a bowl of rice or stir-fry, it is the toasty, savoury, vegetal equivalent of finishing a pasta dish or gratin with Parmesan and breadcrumbs. Sanchi is an easily found brand.

Sansho Often referred to as Japanese green pepper (because of the colour), sansho is actually ground-up prickly ash seed, whatever that is. All I know is that it has a rather marvellous, mysterious flavour and I like it sprinkled on rice.

Chilli pepper blends An increasing number of food producers are launching condiments based on chillies and/or Asian flavourings. Our village health food shop sells an organic Red Hot Chilli Blend that combines red chillies, black pepper, sweet peppers, ginger and ginseng. The bottle has its own built-in grinder (clever idea) and the contents deliver a violent punch: I suspect I am in danger of using it rather too frequently.

getting STARTED

The reason you are fat is because you eat more food than your body needs. Admit this and you're on the way to doing something about it – unlike Mrs Scott, a woman I was talking to recently. Actually, she looked fantastic: tall, full-bosomed, with elegantly coiffed, copper-bright hair and a sheer, full-length leopard-print gown. She showed me photographs to prove that she hadn't always been fat. Her current weight problem, she explained, was entirely medical. I nodded politely, while not believing a word of it: very few people are fat because of a thyroid deficiency or any other medical problem. The vast majority of us are fat because we eat too damned much and don't do enough to use up the number of calories we have consumed.

I find the best way to kick-start a diet is to spend a week in a health clinic, but while that certainly helps, it is utterly worthless in the long run if you aren't seriously motivated to continue. From bitter experience I can tell you quite categorically that dieting so you can fit into a size-12 dress on your 40th birthday will not be sufficient reason to sustain a diet for longer than a fortnight or so. Think about it: if you were that concerned about your appearance you wouldn't be fat in the first place. Vanity may not be the most admirable attribute but it certainly prevents those who have it from bulging like Santa's sack. Sadly, I can't help you with finding the necessary motivation because it has to be genuine and fundamental – by which I mean fundamental to you, not to me or anyone else.

Personally, I became seriously concerned about my health. Whichever magazine I picked up, there seemed to be an article relating to menopause and the medical conditions which may accompany or follow it. Without any warning, I had apparently turned from a healthy woman of moderate years into an old crone at the risk of thrombosis, heart failure, breast cancer, ovarian cancer (or any other cancer looking for a billet), late-onset diabetes and fallen arches. What made me really sit up was the research that suggested fat menopausal women were far more vulnerable to these potential illnesses than women of normal weight. The putative health problems I was courting, and a general frustration with my personal circumstances, gradually conjoined – not in a quiet miaow for attention but a massive roar. It was time for a change.

First, I checked into Shrubland Hall, which I'm lucky to have on my door-step. Not all health clinics are as principled. I remember once telling someone about the night-time hot water and lemon regime at Shrublands. "Oh," she said, "at the last health farm I went to, we were given hot chocolate at bed-time." Ridiculous – the only place to drink hot chocolate is at Florian's. Although some of the facilities may be rather more old-fashioned than is desirable, I love the calm atmosphere, the integrity of the treatments and the tenderness of the staff. More importantly, a week at Shrublands is enough to change my eating pattern completely. After an unremitting diet of raw salad, the prospect of a chunk of seared cod with wilted greens becomes a treat, rather than the dietary privation it seems normally. The idea of eating deep-fried fish and chips doesn't enter one's mind.

But anyone genuinely fat has to come to terms with the fact that dieting isn't for a week but for life. Like any other addict, I found the idea of having to think about both the quality and quantity of what I ate, day-in, day-out, utterly depressing – until I realised that had always been the case. All I needed to do was put a different spin on my obsession with food, altering it from one of over-indulgence, self-hatred and despair to one of moderation and serendipity. There was no need to feel bleak about the thought of having to watch what I ate for ever and eternity, I just needed to tackle the issue in a proactive and positive way.

Fat Girl Slim is nothing to do with the quick-fix, lose-five-pounds-to-show-off-your-bikini-in-Marbella style of dieting. Instead it's all to do with eating exuberantly flavoured meals that are spirited and sustaining – food that lashes at the senses but quietens the belly. Along with a bevy of good-tasting recipes, *Fat Girl Slim* is also about the tactics, tricks and ploys I employed (and still do) during my dieting odyssey. Some of them are purely psychological, some of them are practical. You must, for example, keep a 'clean' house. This doesn't mean that the cupboards should be bare (or full of vacuum cleaners). In fact, quite the reverse – fill the buggers until they overflow, but not with food that's going to lead you into profligacy. It's quite impossible to diet when there is a box of Jaffa Cakes in the house. Sooner or later your resolve to ignore them will evaporate and you'll find yourself a thousand calories to the bad. But stash a packet of caramel rice cakes in the cupboard and you can snack with equanimity. Shop wisely but lavishly is my motto.

One last thought: diet talk is immensely boring and a waste of time. So, cut the crap, button your lip (but not so tightly you can't force some salmon teriyaki in between) and just get on with it.

YOUR DIET, not mine

One of the low points in my dieting history was an evening spent at a slimming club. I am not trying to avoid a libel case by omitting the name of the company that owned it, I simply can't remember. I suspect it wouldn't matter anyway, because if these clubs have one thing in common it is a jaw-dropping eschewal of anything that constitutes good food. I'll go further and say that most of them – and their associated magazines – appear to be geared to the lowest common denominator, embracing everything that's bad (and astonishingly old-fashioned) about the British diet.

Looking at a recent feature on how to lose 4 pounds in a week, I could only gape with fascinated revulsion at the recipes. Who in this world would choose to breakfast on a slice of bread (bread, mark you, not even toast) spread with a tablespoon of tomato ketchup? Lunch was almost as scary, and reached a nadir with a sandwich made from wafer-thin slices of turkey – in other words, those damp flaps of reconstituted, unidentifiable poultry pulp – welded together with cranberry sauce, and 'a medium peach'. It didn't specify whether the peach was fresh or canned, but either way it sounds totally repellent. For supper you could have a 'roast dinner' comprising 3 ounces of lean pork, 2 tablespoons of apple sauce, 4 small boiled potatoes and 1 teaspoon of low-fat spread. It's difficult to think of anything more bleak, except a corned beef 'bake' with low-fat yoghurt topping.

My reason for sharing this demonstration of gastronomic pond life with you is not merely to feel superior but to make the point that there must be people prepared to eat this kind of rubbish or the magazines wouldn't sell. It was the same at the slimming club where, despite being given a number of diet sheets supposed to satisfy different demands, each one contained a style of food that was not only depressingly downmarket but, oddly enough, quite unhealthy: may I be forced to listen to *Candle in the Wind* for all eternity if I ever come to regard a Strawberry Dream Cake as a 'treat'. It's real food I have a problem with, not garbage.

Regardless of whether the food in this book is 'good' or not, there's no reason why you should share my tastes down to the last stick of liquorice. One man's poison is definitely another man's jar of Marmite – and this is part of the reason why I have shied away from giving any of those rigid daily or weekly menus. Apart from personal taste, what happens if you are away for a couple of days, or have been invited out for lunch, or can't get to a shop that

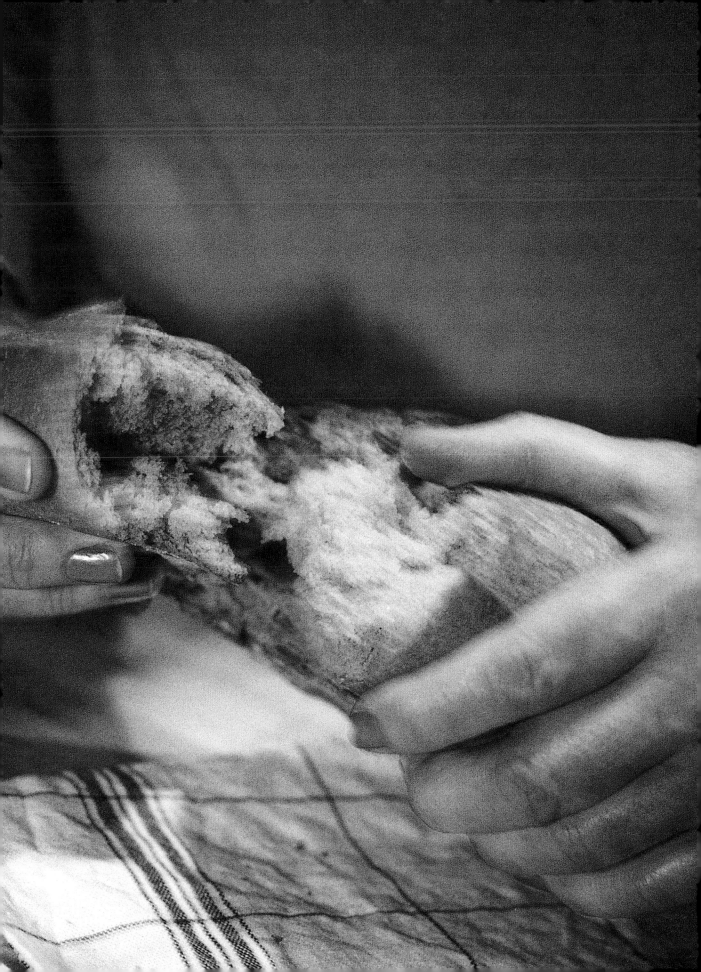

sells rocket, or have a craving for steak that day, or don't feel like cooking, or have a partner who won't eat chicken or... anyway, I have never understood the point of them.

The only way you will succeed in losing weight over a prolonged period is to find a plethora of foods that you, yourself, like. If you slavishly try to follow my diet it simply won't work – particularly if you hate shellfish (prawns pop up in this book more often than Princess Caroline in *Hello!*). I also happen to enjoy a late breakfast of yoghurt mixed with fresh berries, but that doesn't mean you have to like it as well. You must have what you want for breakfast, whether it's grilled bacon and mushrooms or a mango smoothie - and eat it when you like. All I can tell you is what worked for me and try to reassure you that it is possible to eat well and still lose weight. It's up to you to fill in or change the details to suit your own life.

I've already mentioned that a diet will only be successful if it is sustainable. It took me nearly a year to lose four stone and that's a lot longer than 12 months if you are relying on willpower alone. You'll be in even more trouble if you try to follow one of the myriad 'fad' diets for any length of time. Naturally it's possible to give up all fats or all carbohydrates for a few weeks and plenty of people have coped with an unvarying diet of eggs or grapefruit for 10 days or so. But these diets are not only potentially dangerous, they are also deathly boring – and, apparently, cause a veritable cesspool of farting, burping and bad breath. There is no escaping the fact that humans have been designed as omnivores and I really believe it's important to retain as many food groups in one's diet as possible. Certainly, once the euphoria of losing a few pounds has dissipated, there needs to be more than an unwavering prospect of soup, soup and more soup to keep one going.

For me, there was only one food I felt I needed to eliminate and that was, and still is, bread. The problem is I adore the stuff.

It has always been something I love to chew and find impossible to eschew. It's not even that I smother bread with lashings of butter or load it with gooey cheese: I am more than happy to rip a floury shard straight from the loaf and eat it naked and true. The horrible fact is that if my daily allowance of 1200kcal excludes bread I will lose weight, but if it includes bread I will stay the same or, worse, put some pounds on.

Fortunately for my sanity, and your disbelief, recent research supports this apparent nonsense. First, it is common knowledge that ingesting carbohydrate affects our blood and the level of insulin contained in it. (Insulin is the hormone that carries glucose to our muscles and regulates our fat metabolism.) The more carbohydrate we eat, the more insulin enters our bloodstream and the more fat is stored in our tissues. Normally the fat is burned off when the insulin level drops, but what scientists have now discovered is that if we continue to eat carbohydrate the insulin level stays raised and the fat remains stored. In other words, carbohydrate helps the metabolism to retain fat.

Now, I am not for one second suggesting that you completely cut out bread (or any other healthy carbohydrate such as potatoes or pasta) from your diet. All I know is that for me, at least, eating bread hinders rather than helps me lose weight. My solution is to have a dedicated bread day, once a month. Of course it's got to be really good bread, either a huge slab of hand-made rosemary, olive oil and sea salt focaccia or a loaf of tough, chewy, crusty sourdough. I don't need anything with the focaccia but I may have a smear of jam or a scraping of first-rate unsalted butter on the sourdough. The thing to remember is that I will eat bread, and only bread, on that day: I won't top it up with a mushroom omelette in the evening. That way I can really enjoy, indeed luxuriate, in the pleasure of eating something I adore without suffering any pangs of guilt or remorse.

I am not nearly so fanatical about restricting fat intake, although neither does this mean I espouse the Atkins pound-of-cheese-a-day doctrine. But I refuse to join the fat mafia led by the supermarkets, who are always keen to jump on a populist bandwagon if it's to their commercial advantage. Basically I count calories and, as fat is highly calorific, this means that it doesn't get too much of a look-in: I am quite happy to start a big stir-fry with a tablespoon of oil but I am not prepared to splurge nearly a quarter of my daily allowance on two tablespoons of mayonnaise. I realise the notion of counting calories probably sounds tedious, if not impossible, but I only keep a rough tally. Anyway, I don't believe there's a woman alive who doesn't know that biscuits, cake, crisps, pork pie, sausages, sweets, chocolate, milk shakes, hamburger, chips, curry, cream sauces, booze and cucumber are stacked to the gunwales with the blighters. (Okay, I threw the last one in to make sure you were still concentrating.)

(And I say women rather than men, because I am convinced most chaps don't really want to know what's in food. Why else why would my husband persist in eating huge quantities of macaroni cheese washed down with a couple of bottles of Bud at the same time as telling me he wants to lose weight? He also seems to think that Snickers and Revels enjoy a mystical calorie-free status.)

Although I keep a weather eye out for fat and 'bad' carbohydrates (the sugary sort contained in biscuits), I am not unduly concerned about the calorie content of much else, especially fruit and vegetables. With the obvious exception of bananas and potatoes (high in starch) and avocados (high in 'good' fat), I count anything that comes out of the ground or grows on a tree or a bush as 'free'. Undoubtedly this means there are days when I eat more than 1200kcal, but then again there are probably days when I eat less. Anyway, it's a damned sight healthier succumbing to the sweet allure of a banana than that of a chocolate éclair – and I did lose 4 stone in nearly a year, so I must have got something right.

I may be careless about counting the calories in a box of blueberries, but I do try to balance out the protein, carbohydrate and fat elements of my diet over the course of a day. If I have scrambled eggs for lunch then I won't have too much protein for supper but will stick to soup or vegetables and a bit of carbohydrate. Conversely, if lunch has been a big bowl of Japanese rice with seaweed, toasted seeds and soy, then I'll have chicken or fish for supper, always with lots of vegetables. Fruit, regardless of its natural sugar content, is an all-day and all-evening love affair. I couldn't live without it, which is why I find dieting so much easier in the summer: black cherries (not those bland, squashy Turkish ones but firm, crisp English or American cherries) go some way towards satisfying my craving for Maltesers. I also try to leave a quota of at least 500kcal for my evening meal, because that's the one I share with my husband and the one I care about the most. But, I repeat, both pace and content have to suit your lifestyle, not mine, so if you prefer to eat more lavishly at lunchtime then do.

Another small but very important factor in my diet is remembering not to eat everything on my plate, simply because it's there. I say 'remember' because the act of eating is so often automatic, rather than conscious.

And, in my case, the combined doctrine of a rations-weary mother whose mantra was not to waste food, and a philanthropic boarding school that banged on endlessly about starving African children, ensured that any thought of leaving food on my plate was anathema. The trouble is that if you don't want to be fat you must sometimes do just that. Over the last year I've become quite adept at taking one bite of a chocolate or biscuit and throwing the rest away. It helps having a couple of dogs to hoover up the remnants, too, although in Jessie's case I have to watch her waistline even more ferociously than my own. But rest assured no amount of Ethiopian children will ever benefit from whether you leave the biscuit that comes with your coffee, or not, so don't feel guilty about 'wasting' food.

I am also very conscious of my danger zones, temporally. I nearly always come adrift

around five o'clock, apparently the time when most of us are at a physiological low point. Then (and sometimes very late at night), I start prowling around the house, stricken with a rampant desire to scoff myself silly, preferably with something sweet. Your danger zone may occur at a different time, but an important part of dieting successfully is to recognise and acknowledge that there will (not may) be times of the day when you will want to eat, not in a normal, controlled fashion, but in a clamouring jangle of sugar-seeking desperation. Whatever you do, don't ignore this phenomenon. Make sure the house is stacked with saintly but appealing foods that you can nibble on with a degree of impunity. Willpower will not see you through, food will.

Equally, you should not ignore or exclude any food to which you are devoted or even addicted. Bread may not be your own *bête noire* but you may want to devise a way of incorporating ice cream, chocolate, potatoes or wine into your diet. If anything has an unreasonable grip on your psyche, don't think it can be controlled by mental resolution or the thrill of visible weight loss: sooner or later the beast will rear its ugly head, so you may as well be fully primed and ready to tame it. I prefer to embrace the whole-hog philosophy of dieting, viz. my blow-out bread day, but if you think a little bit of what you fancy is a better model then don't let me stop you. For your diet to succeed you must find your own gastronomic lexicon.

I've mentioned wine, and it has to be said that many people find it far harder to forgo alcohol than food. This is not a gender issue – both my husband, David, and a lovely fat girlfriend of mine would far rather go without food than they would a glass (or four) of wine. Unfortunately, while chocolate éclairs yell out their unsuitability, a virginal-looking vodka and tonic tends to be far less vociferous. But alcohol is stuffed full of calories and glugging it unwittingly swells the stomach big-time. As my obsession is for bread, not wine, I asked David how he coped with the problem. He suggested a number of tactics, the first being to use a smaller wine glass (125ml rather than 175ml, for example). We all tend to down what's in the glass, regardless of its size, so if the unit is not as big it helps. This technique echoes my own habit of breaking up a big bar of chocolate into smaller chunks, so I know it makes sense.

The next trick is always to have a glass of water to hand if you are drinking a glass of wine. Again, I understand the benefit of this ploy from occasions when I am the driver, and therefore not drinking. I realised a long time ago that I continually reach for a glass when I am eating. If I've only got one glass and it's full of wine, that's what I'll drink. If I've got two, and one is full of water, then I'm as happy to drink that. The point is that it's not alcohol, *per se*, that I crave, but liquid. I do think it's quite important to make the water interesting, though. I can't stand Suffolk tap water, so I always drink Badoit – I like its slightly salty flavour. But even if your tap water is quite palatable, it's still worth investing in a few cases of (over-priced, I know) sparkling water. If you can build the water habit into your domestic arrangements, and not just when you're out, you'll find that your alcohol intake will be halved – quite literally.

It also matters what type of wine you drink. First, it's much easier to glug white wine than red, but you could always turn the former into a spritzer. Use something like Vinho Verde or Moselle, or anything that's low in alcohol but has enough character to survive dilution. Make sure the wine is very cold (you don't want to add ice) and top it up with soda water or a neutral-flavoured sparkling water. Half wine to half water is about right. Another technique for reducing alcohol consumption is to drink a really good vintage wine rather than an everyday quaffing wine. It's not only the cost that stops people downing a bottle of 1949 claret at one fell swoop but the fact that fabulous wine demands to be sipped, savoured and lingered over. And, psychologically, it's a lot easier to leave half a bottle of vintage wine for drinking up the next day than a glug-glug type of wine.

How you cope with domestic drinking is relatively easy compared to social drinking. If the uppermost thought in your head is to reassure your host that you are not a party-pooper then the safest ploy by far is to say you are driving – whether you are or not. No one in this day and age will demur when you refuse any alcohol. It's a little harder if it's yourself that you are trying to dupe. A spritzer is one answer, and so is a spicy Virgin Mary, but it's also surprising how festive fizzy mineral water cut with fruit juice (preferably something sour or bitter, such as cranberry) and loads of ice can taste. I'm not going to give recipes here, but next time you're in a fashionable bar, check out the array of non-alcoholic drinks on the cocktail list. If you still don't buy into this trickery, I have one more ace up my sleeve. It's something I do myself and it's dead simple: I stick a single shot of vodka (or whatever) into every third or fourth 'innocent' drink. It's enough to prevent me from feeling like a teetotal wallflower and adds a faint hint of danger to the proceedings – very faint.

There's one last thing you need to know about alcohol, and it may explain why people who continue to drink find it very difficult to lose weight – even though they don't eat very much. I am not a scientist and only learned this recently, but apparently the body takes the line of least resistance when it comes to converting what you eat and drink into energy. The simplest molecules provide the most direct route for conversion and as alcohol is one of the smallest hydrocarbon molecules that's what the body picks first. So, if you eat as well as drink a fair bit, you're likely to build up quite a store of unspent calories – hence no weight loss.

As I've said, it's not alcohol that presents me with a problem but food. Whatever your own predilection, it won't alter the three central principles that are necessary for dieting success. Firstly, if you are going to be able to carry on after the initial euphoria of losing a few pounds your diet must limit as few food groups as possible – in other words, it should not be faddy. Secondly, it must suit you and the way you live your life: deny your natural desire for certain foods and/or adopt a punitive eating regime at your peril. Finally, it's important to recognise that it's not just your stomach that needs to be satisfied, but your palate. Bags of flavour and a good mouth-feel – the physical sensation engendered by ingesting different textures – are imperative. Eating a relentless diet of salad, for example, won't do anything to quell the longing for something robust and chewy.

As the months of my own diet progressed I became aware that there were certain dishes that never failed to satisfy on all counts, however regularly I ate them. It's no accident that they contain fantastically savoury flavours, multi-textural contrasts and sheer bulk, all within one bowl. It's all to do with umami (see page 62). To anyone who shares my love of Asian-style food, huge quantities of vegetables and – dare I say – tofu, I commend the following recipes.

Muddled crab and oyster sauce + fragrant rice

It's not just the canning process that makes tinned crab (mostly from Thailand) pretty pointless: warm-water shellfish rarely has the concentrated sweet edge of cold northern-water crustacea. But I do love the vigorous, messy, flavour-saturated way in which they deal with fish in the Far East. Now you can buy fresh white crabmeat already picked it's not difficult to put together a fairly convincing Asian-style dish. The quantity of crab you use depends more on your pocket than either calories or appetite. Being very piggy, I'd go for the larger quantity but this gorgeous muddle will still taste very good if less is used.

ingredients for 2

150g Thai fragrant rice

1 tbsp groundnut oil

1 mild red or green chilli
de-seeded and finely chopped

2 garlic cloves
crushed and finely chopped

2 large flat chestnut mushrooms
cut into large bite-sized chunks

1 'thumb' of root ginger
peeled and grated

about 75ml oyster sauce

1 tbsp dark soy sauce

125–225g fresh white crab meat

a pencil-thick bundle of chives
finely chopped

Pour the rice into a measuring jug and note the volume. Wash off the starch by rinsing the rice in a sieve under cold running water for 2 minutes then tip it into a medium-sized saucepan with double the volume of cold water and a good pinch of salt. Cover the pan and bring the rice to a boil. Give it a quick stir then simmer over a low heat for about 10 minutes, or until a grain of rice is tender to the teeth. Pull the pan aside, put a folded tea towel under the lid and leave it in a warm place.

Meanwhile, heat the oil in a large non-stick wok over a medium-high flame. Add the chilli and garlic and fry for 1 minute, stirring, then add the mushrooms and ginger. Continue stir-frying for 2 minutes, or until the mushrooms have wilted a little, then add the oyster and soy sauces. Reduce the heat to low-medium, stir well and cook for 3 minutes more. Stir in the crab meat and chives and cook for 1–2 minutes, or until the crab is hot. Divide the rice between two big bowls and spoon the crab mixture on top. Serve immediately.

more lucky you – you can have two-thirds of the rice.
less sorry – you'll have to make do with the rest.

Pot-roast chicken + cabbage, morels and squash

A friendly, wintry number this, chunk-full of good flavour and texture, and amenable to casual, unskilled cooking. If dried morels are not available, use (about 175g) strongly flavoured shiitake or dark field mushrooms, chopped into large chunks: ordinary button mushrooms are not man enough. As you won't have the soaking liquid (from the morels) use 500ml of water and 2 teaspoons of stock powder instead. Similarly, you can substitute 1 finely chopped fresh red chilli for the chipotle – although the latter does add an intriguing flavour.

ingredients for 2+

1 tbsp olive oil

1 large onion
cut into large dice

2–3 garlic cloves
crushed and roughly chopped

1 smallish organic chicken

1 'thumb' of root ginger
peeled and grated

20g dried morels
soaked in 500ml hot water for 20 minutes

1 chipotle (dried jalapeño chilli)
soaked with the mushrooms

1 small butternut squash
peeled and cut into large bite-sized chunks

1 small Savoy cabbage
trimmed, quartered, cored and sliced crossways into thin ribbons

Preheat the oven to 140°C fan/gas mark 3. Heat the oil in a cast-iron casserole over a medium flame. Tip in the onion and garlic and fry for about 5 minutes, stirring occasionally, until they have slightly softened. Push the veg to one side and turn up the heat a fraction. Put in the chicken and quickly colour it on all sides, then remove the casserole from the heat.

Add the ginger to the casserole, then strain in the mushroom soaking liquid. Chop the mushrooms roughly and the chilli finely, and add them too. Tuck the squash around the chicken and season fairly generously.

Put the casserole back on the stove, covered, and bring the liquid to a boil. Immediately transfer it to the oven and cook the chicken for 40 minutes, then lift it out and stir in the cabbage. Replace the chicken the other way up and continue to cook for 20–30 minutes, or until the cabbage has wilted and the chicken juices run clear when you stab a skewer into the thickest part of the thigh. Leave the casserole in a warm place, still covered, for 15 minutes before serving.

more mashed potato, of course, with plenty of butter, milk and black pepper.
less the squash is all the carbohydrate you need.

Pot-luck veg

If you toss enough interesting vegetables together with masses of Asian flavourings, I defy even the most raven carnivore to notice the absence of meat. By all means alter the veg to suit your own taste but don't leave out the mushrooms as they provide an earthy substance. As with all stir-fries, it's vital to keep everything moving.

ingredients for 2

I tbsp groundnut (or vegetable) oil

I medium onion
chopped into small dice

2 leeks
topped, tailed and the dark-green part discarded, then halved lengthways and sliced into long, thickish ribbons

3 garlic cloves
crushed and finely chopped

I red chilli
de-seeded and finely chopped

**125g exotic mixed mushrooms
(e.g. shiitake, oyster mushrooms etc)**
roughly broken

2 courgettes
cut into medium dice

I 'thumb' of root ginger
peeled and grated

I stick of lemon grass
inner leaves only, finely chopped

3 heads of pak choi
cut into double bite-sized chunks

3 big handfuls of spring greens
tough stalks discarded, the leaves sliced into thin ribbons

500ml shiitake broth
made up as instructed on the bottle

2 tbsp Thai fish sauce (nam pla)

2–3 tbsp Japanese soy sauce

I (75g) bundle of fine rice noodles

Heat a large non-stick wok over a medium-high flame, then add the oil. Throw in the onion and leeks, fry them for 2 minutes, then add the garlic and chilli and cook for I minute. Toss in the mushrooms and courgettes, and fry for 2 minutes. Add the ginger, lemon grass, pak choi and spring greens, and fry for 2 minutes. Pour in the shiitake broth, fish and soy sauces, and bring to a boil.

Add the noodles and cook for 2 minutes. Remove the wok and set aside for I–2 minutes, or until the noodles are tender. Return the wok to a high heat and serve as soon as the broth begins to bubble again.

WORKING
woman's REALITY

How does the saying go? Breakfast like a king and dine like a pauper? Well, as far as I'm concerned it's an unattainable counsel of perfection because I have never ever been able to stomach any food until at least three hours after opening my eyes. As a child I could just about manage to down a mug of Bournvita (ice-cold milk, and chocolate granules barely dissolved) before going off to school. The situation hadn't much improved by the time I was going out to work in my early twenties, except that I was prepared to tackle the odd bowl of (raw) porridge sprinkled with brown sugar, again tempered with ice-cold milk. Only a little, mind you – any innate fondness for the stuff was quickly scotched by compulsory school milk, and the evil habit teachers had of storing it by the radiator. Hot milk is bad enough but tepid milk is like warm octopus semen. (How would I know? Because I was a cephalopod hooker in a previous incarnation, of course.)

My eating pattern has not changed much through the passing years. Despite endless magazine articles promulgating the benefits of an early breakfast, it's still mid-morning before the first food passes my lips. Because breakfast is late, lunch topples into tea time, and dinner is whenever I stop writing and/ or my husband comes home. This can be a fairly civilised eight o' clock, but if we're both working in our restaurant it's more likely to be nigh-on midnight before we have our evening meal. A nutritionist's nightmare, I think you'll agree, but here's the strange thing: it doesn't seem to make a blind bit of difference to how much weight I gain or lose. Of course, I can see that eating earlier must make sense but I am living proof that irregular eating habits should not be used as an excuse for either piling on the pounds or retaining them.

As a rule, I prefer yoghurt and fruit first thing in the morning – or even last thing in the morning. While my preference is for sheep's milk yoghurt, sod's law decrees that this is the richest of them all, so I save it for a special once-a-month treat. Goat's milk yoghurt contains less fat but, on the whole, I stick to the unashamedly commercial Müller Light yoghurts, preferably those flavoured with vanilla, banana or peach and maracuya. (I'll countenance the idea of yoghurt and toffee sharing the same pot when I see cows wearing woolly cardigans and bouncing little children on their knees.) The texture is a bit gloopy and the flavour lacks

that real lactic kick, but Müller yoghurts are a darned sight better-tasting than most low-fat versions. (In fact, one highly reputable food retailer sells an own-brand product that I swear should be in the DIY section.) Anyway, if I am feeling particularly gloomy about its banality, I sometimes liven it up with a spoonful or two of tangy, locally made yoghurt. I normally add a carton of raspberries, blackberries or blueberries too – although a sliced fresh peach, nectarine or mango can be equally felicitous. A small sliced banana with a (very) few snippets of stem ginger or a pinch or two of toasted seeds is also jolly good. (A tip from the Packet Queen, see page 52, leave fruits such as berries, grapes or cherries sealed in their plastic cartons when you rinse them. Most packaging is perforated with holes or slits and you can simply hold the box under the cold tap, then shake it to drain off the water.)

Occasionally I ring the changes with a bowl of cereal – but not very often because of my (unsubstantiated) belief that wheat provokes mild indigestion and then hangs around my body like a millstone (an unplanned but appropriate metaphor). Sometimes I munch on my old favourite, raw porridge, although nowadays I only eat organic oats. Or I may push the boat out and have a bowl of Grape Nuts. Either way I'll use a minimum of milk and let the dogs finish whatever hasn't been mopped up by the cereal. To cap off my imperfect breakfast, I then make myself a perfect double espresso using Illy coffee and my trusty Dualit espresso machine.

My dietary transgressions don't stop at breakfast: I also eat lunch at my desk. I know we're all meant to leap to our feet at midday and dash off to the park to breathe fresh air and nibble a wholesome salad, but I don't and never have. That tedious Protestant work ethic with which I'm cursed (weird, since my mother is anything but God-fearing) fills me with a permanent sense of guilt if I'm not constantly labouring. Recent research indicates that increasingly fewer people are going out for lunch, or even taking a full hour's break. Well, that's nothing new for me. When I feel hungry I just make a quick trip to the kitchen and come straight back to my desk. Lunch is eaten in between the clicking of a mouse and the clattering of a keyboard – in fact, I'm writing these precise words in between bites of smoked trout fillet, sliced avocado, grated carrot with lime juice, and a pinch of toasted sesame seeds.

The important thing to remember is that being stuck at a desk for a long period guarantees you'll want to pick, so it helps to make lunch a really long, straggly affair. You may not want to mix paperwork with peeling a pile of prawns (see page 131) but you can load your plate with a whole sliced cucumber that can be eaten slice by painstaking slice. Or have a large carton of tiny tomatoes or a big plate of paper-thin melon slices to hand. I also keep a stock of chewing gum, Corn Thins and a bag of dried figs close by (the figs not to be scoffed in one sitting but nibbled at daintily). And don't forget to drink. There's always a bottle of Badoit and a glass on my desk and every time I want to eat I have a gulp of water instead.

It's astonishing how you can kill a couple of desperate hours with fluid instead of food. Unlike smoking, drinking water is good for you but, like smoking, it gives your hands (and brain) something to do.

Of course I realise that not everyone has the privilege of conducting their business at home. (And, indeed, there may even be a few house-parents reading this who are wondering when I'm going to acknowledge their presence: sorry – hello.) For many years I commuted into London and I know that unless you take a packed lunch into work it's jolly hard to eat healthily. Most sandwiches are welded together with oodles of mayonnaise and the selection of ones that are not is pretty paltry – it doesn't take long for the allure of plain roast chicken sarnies to pall. The incursion of sushi into the lunchtime snack culture helps, as does the proliferation of soup bars, but it still isn't easy. As for fruit, I don't think a bowl of warm, woolly imported apples sitting by the till counts. Even if you are able to shop for proper ingredients – and have an office kitchen equipped with a hot plate or microwave – there's no doubt it requires serious endeavour to maintain a diet while out at work. The only saving grace may be that other colleagues are also trying to eat healthily: the concept of safety in numbers is particularly pertinent in a dieting context, hence the proliferation of slimming clubs.

While I may be particularly lucky in working from home and having access to a decent kitchen, it's not all plain sailing: I still have to contend with the cheese sandwich menace. It's quite simple – all my life, cheese sandwiches have been my default working lunch because a) they are quick to make, b) the ingredients are to hand, c) I don't like meat very much,

d) I love cheese with a passion, e) I love bread with even more of a passion. Breaking out of this lunchtime habit has been one of my greatest achievements. There's no mystery or clever sleight of hand involved – I stopped buying bread and I stopped buying cheese.

Without this former mainstay my midday eating now divides fairly evenly between knocking up something made from fresh ingredients, such as scrambled eggs, or opening up a packet. You may think it odd that a food writer and restaurateur could even contemplate buying ready-prepared food. Well, I'm not proud of this fiercely expensive (pro rata) habit but, unlike many of my colleagues, I live in the real world – one that doesn't have a bevy of fantastic food shops all a stone's throw from my door. Our village shop has a huge selection of crisps and soft drinks, but not much in the way of fresh fruit and veg. The nearest farmshop is 20 minutes away and, reasonably, is only at its best during the fairly short growing season. The local farmers' market is a half-hour's drive and is only held monthly – in fact, you can find fresher, more interesting winter vegetables in Islington on a Sunday morning than in Suffolk all week. As for taking food from our restaurant kitchen, I don't. (There are a number of reasons not pertinent to this book, but you are welcome to email me if you want to know more.) Most significantly, I don't have one job but two or three, depending on whether I am writing a book or not. I don't march to the beat of my own drum: I stumble around to the cacophony of everyone else's. At 8 o' clock in the evening, tired and hungry, I am afraid I don't want to cook, I just want to eat.

You've heard it all a million times before, but what you really mustn't do is to starve yourself during the day. While I may not embrace the big breakfast philosophy as wholeheartedly as I should, I do realise that it's utterly stupid to avoid eating anything at all until the evening. All that happens, believe me, is a feeding frenzy more violently charged than a rugby team at a free buffet. By all means keep the calorie count down so you can enjoy a fairly carefree dinner with your partner, but make sure you carry on nibbling – and drinking water – throughout the day. If all else fails, take on a job that requires pristine fingers (turning pages for a pianist) or keeps you in the public eye (auctioneer) or requires an empty mouth (radio presenter). Drastic measures, but worth considering.

Warm mushroom and prawn salad

This is dead simple, extremely quick and will taste even better if you use whole Greenland prawns and peel them yourself. (I realise this is not something you may want to do during a working day, but consider peeling them the night before, when you have more time. As a guide, 225g of shell-on prawns produce about 85g peeled prawns – and the debris makes brilliant shellfish stock.) Mushrooms are peculiarly accommodating, especially teamed with fish and shellfish, and this makes as good a starter as it does a snack.

ingredients for 1

1 tbsp groundnut (or vegetable) oil

1 celery stick
cut into small dice

2 garlic cloves
finely sliced

85g button mushrooms
wiped clean and larger ones halved

about 225g shell-on Greenland prawns
peeled

a small handful of parsley
chopped

**a handful of mixed salad leaves
including watercress**

Heat a medium non-stick frying pan set over a low-medium flame. Add the oil, then throw in the celery and garlic and, stirring frequently, cook them for about 3 minutes or until the garlic begins to colour.

Tip in the mushrooms and add a generous amount of seasoning. Cook the mushrooms for 3–4 minutes, or until they have just wilted, stirring frequently. Add the prawns and parsley, and let everything heat through for 1–2 minutes, stirring occasionally.

Put the salad leaves on a serving plate and pour over the contents of the frying pan, including all the juices. Eat immediately.

more if you decide to serve this as a starter, the mixture is particularly good spooned over slices of toasted ciabatta, when it becomes prawn and mushroom bruschetta.

Jazzed-up scrambled eggs on mushrooms

Scrambled eggs on toast is one of my all-time favourite comfort foods. I am not going to pretend that flat mushrooms provide the same wonderful buttery, soft scrunch as toast, but with their deeply savoury meatiness, they ain't bad. Ring the changes with chunks of (peeled, de-seeded) tomatoes; griddled courgette, asparagus or aubergine; wilted spinach or rocket; or anything else that makes sense with eggs (except cheese).

ingredients for 1

a few purple sprouting broccoli stems
tough old stalks trimmed off and discarded

2 large flat chestnut mushrooms
wiped clean

(optional) a dash of mushroom ketchup or Worcestershire sauce

a little olive oil

a scrap of butter

1 garlic clove
crushed and finely chopped

1 mild red chilli
de-seeded and finely chopped

3 large free-range eggs
whisked just long enough to combine

1 (tinned) piquillo pepper
cut into small dice

2–3 anchovy fillets
roughly chopped

Preheat the grill. Bring a saucepan of salted water to a boil over a high flame. Throw in the broccoli and cook it, uncovered, for about 3 minutes, or until just tender. Drain and chop the stems into 2 or 3 and keep them warm. Put the mushrooms in the grill pan, skin-side down. Season, then sprinkle them with mushroom ketchup or Worcestershire sauce, followed by some olive oil. Put the pan under the grill – not too close – and cook the mushrooms for about 5 minutes, or until tender. (Because the mushrooms haven't been dowsed in fat, they will probably look a bit dry. Don't worry – the flavour will not be affected and the eggs will cover any wrinkles.)

Meanwhile, melt the butter in a medium non-stick saucepan over a low heat. Add the garlic and chilli, and cook gently for about 2 minutes. Season the eggs with a little salt and lots of pepper, then pour them into the pan. Whisking almost continuously, gently scramble the eggs. It should take at least 5 minutes if the eggs are going to be creamy rather than hard, so reduce the heat if they are forming curds too quickly. When the eggs are thick but still pourable, stir in the piquillo pepper and anchovies. Pull away the pan while the eggs are still not quite set and very gently fold in the broccoli: it will do its damnedest to disintegrate. Put the mushrooms on a warm serving plate, pile on the eggs and eat immediately.

Smoked fish + Japanese rice

I don't often eat hot food at lunchtime, but occasionally I fancy some soup or a bowl of Japanese rice mingled with smoked fish and lots of seasoning. The latter may sound faintly austere but it's all the more beautiful for its simplicity. I like to add smoked trout to the rice but I sometimes toss in a couple of fragmented smoked mackerel fillets instead – and I don't worry about the fat content because they contain the polyunsaturated fatty acid, omega-3, which is good for everyone and particularly menopausal women. Anyway, mackerel is so rich that having to be a bit niggardly isn't a problem.

When samphire is in season (late spring and summer), a handful of blanched, chopped saline-sweet sprigs makes a fantastic addition, but otherwise I am happy to stir in some lightly cooked broccoli sprigs, asparagus or pak choi. The vegetables can be at room temperature rather than piping hot – but not straight from the fridge. Or, I simply scatter roughly chopped herbs, such as chives, parsley or coriander, over the rice.

ingredients for 1

100g Japanese rice
thoroughly rinsed for 2–3 minutes
under cold running water

a handful of blanched samphire
coarse hairy stalks trimmed off

about 100g smoked trout fillets
roughly broken into large shards

2–3 dashes of Japanese soy sauce

**a few shakes of furikake seasoning
(or toasted sesame seeds)**

**(optional) sansho pepper or
Red Hot Chilli Blend**

Drain the rice and tip it into a medium saucepan. Add 150ml cold water and a good pinch of salt, then cover the pan and bring to a boil over a medium-high flame. Immediately reduce the heat and stir the rice thoroughly to disturb any grains that have stuck to the bottom. (The crusty layer that forms on the bottom of the pan is considered a great treat in Japan.) Cover the rice again and simmer it for about 10 minutes, or until all the water has evaporated, and when you bite into a grain it is just about tender. (Japanese rice is meant to cohere slightly, but the individual grains should not be mushy.) If you have time, place a folded tea towel between the lid and the pan and leave the rice for 5 minutes to fluff up.

While the rice is cooking, put the samphire and bits of smoked trout into the bottom of the serving bowl you have left to warm. Pile the rice into the bowl and gently toss it with chopsticks or a fork. Swish on the soy sauce, then sprinkle the rice with furikake and sansho pepper (or black pepper, but not both) and serve immediately.

Mrs Klein's tuna fish salad

You probably think it very odd that I suggest using tuna packed in oil rather than less fattening brine. There is a good reason – it tastes better. To negate the higher calorie count, drain the tuna very well, then tip it on to folded kitchen paper and blot off all the excess oil. I should also explain that while tuna fish salad is commonplace, not to mention banal (especially when used as a supermarket sandwich filling), it's a very different kettle of fish when made with chunky raw vegetables and a degree of brio. My ex-boss's American wife – and long-time friend – introduced me to proper tuna fish salad and I've never looked back. This recipe includes a couple of my own twists and, sadly for the dieter, omits the all-important Kraft Miracle Whip – but it still tastes darned good.

ingredients for 2

1 red pepper
de-seeded and cut into medium dice

2 celery sticks
chopped into medium dice

1 Little Gem lettuce
trimmed and chopped into large bite-sized chunks

¼ cucumber
de-seeded and cut into medium dice

1 (400g) can of cannellini beans
drained and rinsed under cold water

a small handful of parsley
leaves roughly chopped

a small handful of fresh coriander
leaves roughly chopped

1 (about 200g) can of tuna in oil
well drained and excess oil blotted up

3–4 tbsp fat-reduced hummus

**2–3 tbsp Kraft Miracle Whip
(or similarly synthetic-tasting mayo)**

Combine everything in a large bowl except the tuna, hummus and mayo, and season generously. Tip half the mixture into a second bowl. Divide the tuna between both bowls.

more add 2 tablespoons of the mayo to one of the bowls and toss everything together very gently. If more mayo is required to bind the mixture – but not render it too claggy – add a little more. Serve the salad on toasted rye bread or stuffed into warm pitta bread pouches.
less let the hummus down with a little water or vegetable stock until thickly pourable, then pour two-thirds into the dieter's bowl and toss everything together very gently. If it needs more dressing to coat and lightly bind the ingredients, add the rest. Eat the salad as it is or scoop it up with crisp chicory leaves.

Chilled Japanese noodles

Eating a bowl of cold noodles is not for the faint-hearted, but it's as normal to the Japanese as macaroni cheese is to us. (Now that's something I haven't had for a few years... mmmm.) Suspend your natural disbelief and give this recipe a go. Apart from the brilliant, clean, cool taste (which sounds disturbingly like a Sixties ad for menthol cigarettes) the noodles have the added virtue of being able to endure up to 48 hours in the fridge and still emerge unscathed. I normally make two portions, as here, and save one for the following day.

ingredients for 2

300ml boiling water

4 tbsp Japanese soy sauce

3 tbsp mirin

2 tsp caster sugar

2 pinches of dashi stock powder

1–2 tsp made-up wasabi

250g soba (100% buckwheat) noodles

1 sheet of nori (seaweed)

2 spring onions
trimmed and finely sliced

Put the boiling water, soy, mirin and sugar into a saucepan and bring to a boil over a medium-high flame, stirring frequently at the start to dissolve the sugar. Whisk in the dashi powder and, when it has dissolved, remove the pan from the heat. Whisk in the wasabi, to taste, then leave the dashi stock to cool, refrigerating it if necessary.

Bring a very large saucepan of lightly salted water to a boil. Plunge in the noodles and stir thoroughly to make sure they have separated. Bring the water back to the boil and cook the noodles, uncovered, for about 5 minutes, or until just tender. Drain and sloosh them under running cold water until completely rinsed free of starch. Leave the noodles to one side or refrigerate them if you are saving some for the next day.

Holding the sheet of nori in a pair of long-handled tongs, waft it gently over a low flame for a few seconds, until crisp and very lightly toasted on both sides. Scissor the sheet into short strips.

To serve, put the noodles into a deep bowl and pour over enough dashi stock to cover, then strew some nori and spring onions on top. Use chopsticks to muddle the ingredients together and then slurp up the noodles as noisily as you like.

Springtime scrambled eggs

There's no reason to confine scrambled eggs to the breakfast table. Flavoured with something attractive, such as English asparagus and the fresh mild-mannered garlic available in late spring, they make a subtle, sophisticated and – since I have strayed unwittingly into alliteration – splendid supper (or lunch).

ingredients for 2

a few spears of English asparagus
tough, woody ends cut off

a scrap of unsalted butter

4 cloves of new season's garlic
finely sliced

6 large eggs
whisked just long enough to combine yolks and whites

Bring a saucepan of salted water to a boil and toss in the asparagus. Cook it, uncovered, for 4–5 minutes, or until barely tender to the point of a small knife. Drain the asparagus carefully (I fish it out with tongs) and immediately plunge the spears into ice-cold water to stop the cooking and set the colour. Pat the spears dry with kitchen paper and then cut them into bite-sized pieces, leaving the tips whole.

Put the butter into a heavy non-stick saucepan set over a low flame. When it has melted, toss in the sliced garlic and cook it for about 3 minutes, stirring frequently, until slightly softened but not coloured.

Season the whisked eggs and add them to the pan. Reduce the heat and, whisking almost continuously, gently scramble the eggs. It should take at least 5 minutes if the eggs are going to be creamy rather than hard, so reduce the heat if they are forming curds too quickly. When the eggs are thick but still pourable, add the asparagus, but not the tips. Change from a whisk to a wooden spoon and carry on stirring the eggs for 1–2 minutes. Remove the pan from the heat while the eggs are still very soft-looking and continue to stir for another 30 seconds. Pile the eggs on to serving plates and strew with the reserved tips. Serve immediately.

more toast some sourdough bread, spread it with butter and heap the eggs on top. And, if liked – I don't, diet or no diet – you can stir a slurp of double cream in just before the eggs leave the pan, to make them creamier still.

Omelettes

It's all too easy to be sniffy about omelettes, especially as a vegetarian option, but carefully made they are as joyous and beautiful to eat as anything on God's earth. The secret is in the six golden rules.

First, always use the freshest, most properly brought-up eggs you can find – save the battery ones for hurling at EU agricultural ministers; always use a small, heavy dedicated omelette pan; never wash the pan up – merely wipe it out with kitchen paper; don't add salt until just before cooking the omelette as it breaks down the eggs; use only a small amount of filling – the eggs should be the star of the show: always use a high heat – an omelette should be on the plate within 2 minutes of the eggs touching the pan.

There are zillions of things you can put in an omelette, but please don't. Omelettes are not meant to be the eggy equivalent of a bin-bag. Herbs, crab, shrimps or prawns, little snippets of cooked ham or pancetta, or even some cooked veg, such as asparagus, chicory or red pepper, go very well with eggs. When I'm in a real hurry I have also been known to fold in some very finely sliced raw mushrooms: the only caveat is that while the omelette tastes marvellous, the released juices do look a tad unsightly on the plate – one for private rather than public consumption, perhaps. For a classic omelette fines herbes, use a mixture of chives, tarragon, parsley and chervil, adding the herbs to the whisked eggs only seconds before you make the omelette.

---

ingredients for 1

**3 large eggs
(caveat as above)**
whisked just long enough to combine yolks and whites

a tiny scrap of unsalted butter

a scant handful of your chosen filling

Season the eggs fairly generously. Put the omelette pan over a high flame and, when it is hot, add the butter. As it melts, swirl the butter round the pan and pour in the eggs as soon as the sizzling subsides. The egg that's in contact with the base of the pan will immediately start to set; as it does, draw the curds into the middle of the pan with a fork, allowing more raw egg to flow into the space left. Continue until a low range of moist curds has formed in the centre and there's only a little liquid egg left, then strew the filling over the surface. After 15–20 seconds, remove the pan from the heat.

Using a palette knife, flip the edge of the omelette nearest your hand into the middle. Slide the side furthest away from you on to a plate and gently nudge the first folded side over it to form a nice fat pillow. Eat at once.

Hijiki (black seaweed salad)

Whatever preconceptions you have about eating seaweed, please junk them here and now. I say please, but actually that's an order, not a request. I guarantee that if you didn't know, you really wouldn't have a clue that this slightly chewy, noodly-looking seaweed had anything to do with the stuff washed up on Felixstowe beach. Hijiki makes a great sweetish-savoury starter or you can eat huge bowls of it, like I do, for lunch or supper.

ingredients for 4

1 (25g) packet of hijiki

1 tbsp groundnut (or vegetable) oil

115g carrots
cut into fine strips

500ml made-up dashi stock

4 tbsp Japanese soy sauce

3 tbsp mirin

2 tbsp white sugar

Soak the hijiki in a large volume of cold water for 20–30 minutes – it expands fairly dramatically as it hydrates so use a large bowl or pan. Drain, rinse thoroughly and drain again.

Heat a very large, non-stick frying pan over a medium flame, then add the oil. Tip in the hijiki and carrots, and fry them for 1 minute, stirring and tossing constantly. Add the dashi stock, soy, mirin and sugar, and bring to a boil. Reduce the heat and simmer for 8–10 minutes or until the hijiki is just tender – there should still be some resistance to the bite. (The longer you soak it, the shorter the cooking time.)

Drain the cooking liquid into another pan (leaving the hijiki to cool) and boil over a high heat until reduced to a small puddle. Allow this to cool, then pour it back over the hijiki and mix well. Eat immediately or refrigerate for up to 3 days.

Baked potato + nice stuffings

On paper, baked potatoes don't seem hugely exciting, but they do have value in a slimming diet because they are as easy as pouring milk to cook, comfortingly hot and filling. With plenty of fibre, they are also good for you, especially if there are only vitamins lurking in the skins, and not herbicides. As for which are the best varieties to bake, I find the labelling quite misleading and would avoid Marfona (too sweet), Cara (too boring), and Estima (too watery). Crisp-skinned, fluffy-hearted King Edwards are the best by miles.

The problem, of course, is that baked potatoes are nicest running with rivulets of melted butter – and if there are a couple of plump herby sausages along for the ride, then so much the better. So I wonder whether you'll believe me when I say that cottage cheese can taste almost as good when gussied up with prawns, toasted seeds, Japanese seasonings, strips of roasted red pepper or fresh herbs. (If you even think of pineapple chunks I am disowning you.) Another trick is to dollop on reduced-fat tzatziki with extra chopped spring onions and cucumber stirred in. A spoonful or two of soft fresh goat's cheese let down with a little skimmed milk, then mixed with herbs and finely chopped fresh garlic also hits the spot. The following very simple recipes are two of my other favourites.

ingredients for 1

CORIANDER AND PISTACHIO RAITA

1 tbsp each of chopped fresh coriander, chopped chives and chopped mint

1 small red chilli
de-seeded and finely chopped

1 scant tsp nigella (aka black onion) seeds

1 tbsp shelled raw pistachios
roughly chopped

150g 0% fat Greek yoghurt

Mix everything together and season generously with black pepper and a little salt.

BACON AND AVOCADO MAYO

2 tbsp reduced-fat mayonnaise

1–2 tbsp skimmed milk

the juice of 1 lime

2 tbsp chopped parsley

3 thin strips of ready-cooked streaky bacon
roughly crumbled

½ ripe-but-firm avocado
peeled and cut into small bite-sized chunks

Put the mayo into a small bowl and stir in enough milk to soften the consistency a little. Add seasoning and lime juice to taste, then gently fold in the parsley, bacon and avocado.

Aubergine dip + crudités

Don't judge dips by the commercial stuff that comes in dinky plastic pots. If I were Mexican, I think I could be persuaded to sue: no true salsa tastes like the chemical-ridden, ketchup-textured, foul-tasting gunk that masquerades under that name. And, although the usual carrots and cucumber are good, there are plenty of other vegetal candidates that are happy to take the plunge.

ingredients for 1

1 aubergine

2 garlic cloves
crushed and very finely chopped

a good pinch of ground cumin

1 tbsp olive oil

2 tbsp light tahini

a squeeze of fresh lemon juice, to taste

FOR THE CRUDITÉS

choose a selection from the following:

whole baby carrots, sticks of cucumber, cauliflower florets, cherry tomatoes, artichoke hearts, quartered lettuce hearts, wedges of beetroot, blanched asparagus spears, wedges of roast butternut squash, Belgian chicory leaves, strips of red pepper, celery sticks or blanched sticks of celeriac, raw button mushrooms, thin slices of fennel

Perch the aubergine over a low-medium gas flame, turning it every so often with tongs, until the skin is completely charred and the flesh inside is almost a purée: it will take a good 20 minutes. (Or, roast the aubergine at very high heat to achieve a similar – but not so delightfully smoky – effect.)

Peel off the skin and scrape the soft flesh into a food processor. Add the garlic, cumin, olive oil and tahini, and whizz to a thick sludge. Add some lemon juice and seasoning to taste and, if necessary, 1–2 tablespoons of cold water, to achieve a soft, dipping consistency.

The dip will keep refrigerated for 48 hours. Bring it to room temperature and, if it has thickened up too much (as it surely will), whisk in a little more water before serving.

Hard-boiled eggs + dukkah

Funny things, hard-boiled eggs: you either love 'em or hate 'em – there's no halfway house. I adore them, especially with proper home-made mayonnaise (what!) and anchovies criss-crossed over the top. I also like them in sandwiches, with or without cress, tomatoes or salad, and with or without mayo. The only essential is plenty of black pepper and salt – something which every politically correct supermarket or food manufacturer could usefully learn. (How hypocritical is it that the same companies that trumpet about using less salt in their products are the same ones that push endless streams of fat-filled, highly processed junk at us?)

But back to real food, namely hard-boiled eggs. Actually, 'hard-boiled' is not quite what I mean: the eggs should retain the merest dimple of gooey yolk at their heart. Apart from the obvious salad accompaniments, I like to eat the eggs with the seductive Egyptian nut and spice mixture called dukkah.

For this recipe it's better not to use spanking-fresh eggs as they are more difficult to peel – a week older is better. I always cook six eggs in one go so there are some in the fridge, waiting for me. The dukkah will keep for weeks in a cool airtight container, so make a larger quantity if you prefer.

ingredients for 1+

6 large eggs
at room temperature

FOR THE DUKKAH

4 tbsp sesame seeds

2 tbsp coriander seeds

1 tbsp cumin seeds

30g skinned hazelnuts

Fill a small saucepan with enough water to cover the eggs, then bring it to a boil. Carefully put the eggs into the water, immediately reduce the heat and simmer them for exactly 8 minutes. Put the pan (with the eggs still in it) under cold running water and leave it for 3 minutes to prevent that horrible grey tidemark from forming around the yolks. Peel the eggs and dunk them into the dukkah in between each bite.

To make the dukkah, separately dry-fry the seeds and nuts for 1–2 minutes in a frying pan over a medium flame, shaking the pan occasionally. Mix them together, then grind or crush the mixture into a coarse powder, adding seasoning to taste. (If using an electric grinder, don't over-process, or the mixture will turn oily.)

THE PACKET QUEEN

Although we all have our Pot Noodle moments, I try to apply the same high standards when purchasing 'junk' food as I do for fresh ingredients. Naturally, the better supermarkets tend to sell better ready-meals, but not always. There are plenty of stinkers even in the upmarket ranges. It stands to reason that if something only costs a couple of quid, yet has to deliver a profit for everyone down the line (with transportation, processing and packaging adding fiercely to the overheads), the food quality is going to be pretty low – unless we're talking about a tin of baked beans. And if the meal contains meat or fish, even a high retail price won't guarantee you'll find more than a few chunks of (expensive) protein loitering in amongst the copious quantity of (cheap) sauce. As with any other food shopping, you need to sort carefully through the overwhelming garbage that lines the shelves and examine the ingredients lists with religious zeal.

Although I buy ready-prepared food, don't misunderstand me – not everything in my fridge has been heavily processed in an out-of-town industrial estate. The packets are just as likely to contain unmucked-about Parma ham or fresh pineapple chunks as some low-fat Chinese-style chicken assembly. But with the ready-prepared food I like to do some tweaking, to improve not only the flavour but the texture as well. So much prepared food has a pappy, pre-masticated consistency that adding a bit of bite or crunch is almost mandatory. You'll find some specific serving ideas here, but it's not difficult to think of your own.

Almost anything can be perked up with extra chopped herbs, or you can add finely diced vegetables or a few tiny croutons or toasted seeds, as appropriate. I often whisk in a little (good) stock powder to cartons of so-called fresh soups, and most pasta dishes (for the non-dieter) can do with an extra grating of Parmesan or a bit more olive oil. A good squeeze of lemon or lime juice is another simple way to revive food that has been entombed in a plastic coffin.

Spruced-up vegetable soup

The first so-called 'fresh' soups to appear on the chilled counter were remarkably good, but that was a long time ago. Nowadays much of it is no better than packet soup – it just doesn't keep so long. Faced with such a carton the other night, I managed to transform a gloopy, spiced vegetable soup – all top notes and chilli-heat but curiously lacking in any depth of flavour – into something really quite enjoyable. Use any green vegetables, mushrooms and non-Asian herbs that are in your fridge – you won't need any extra root vegetables: they're cheap and will already be in the soup. Chop or tear the greenery as appropriate and don't cook it for too long or you'll lose the colour and freshness.

ingredients for 2–3

1 (500–600g) carton of 'fresh' vegetable soup

1 tbsp Marigold Swiss vegetable bouillon powder

2 handfuls of fresh or frozen peas

a large handful of fine French beans
topped, tailed and cut in half

1 (420g) can of cannellini beans (or similar)
drained and rinsed

about 150g ready-prepared spinach
checked over and torn roughly into thick ribbons

a large handful of parsley
very roughly chopped

Pour the soup into a large saucepan, then add the stock powder and 500ml water, hot or cold. Heat the soup, stirring occasionally, then add the peas and French beans. Simmer the soup for 6–8 minutes, half-covered.

Uncover the pan and add the cannellini beans. Make sure the soup is still simmering, then cram in the spinach and keep tamping it down into the liquid. As soon as the spinach has wilted, stir in the parsley, check the seasoning, then serve.

more non-dieters can stir grated Parmesan into their soup and/or dunk hunks of bread.
less sorry – have another bowl of soup.

Caesar salad + peas and prawns

I am trying hard to avoid mentioning brand names for one very good reason: the notion of a supermarket stocking a particular line for one week, never mind a year, is as unlikely as a girl wearing blue jeans on her wedding day. The problem is that practically all the supermarkets sell ready-made Caesar salad but only one of them bears any resemblance to the real thing, in my opinion. Needless to say it's Marks & Spencer's (normal rather than reduced-fat) Caesar salad that I like the best. (One of the leading dietary versions has a dressing that tastes like paint stripper – I threw it straight in the bin.)

Although the calorie count for Caesar salad is fairly restrained, it's easy to reduce it even further. But, paradoxically, you can also add extra bits and pieces. This is hard for me to admit, as I've long been highly vocal on the subject of Caesar salad and the need to keep it pure and unadorned, but when you're hungry anything goes (I've found). My current favourite rendition incorporates fresh peas and prawns, but fresh crab, grilled chicken, salmon or fresh tuna, as well as chunks of avocado, asparagus spears or griddled artichoke hearts would be equally good. Ready-shelled fresh peas are available nearly all year round (from Kenya, amongst other places) but, as you'd expect, they are at their sweetest and most tender during the summer months.

ingredients for 1

1 tub of Caesar salad

a good handful of peeled prawns

a good handful of raw fresh peas

1–2 tbsp chopped chives

Tip the salad leaves into a big mixing bowl. (I have a favourite pale blue bowl, made from some kind of synthetic material, that looks suitably American and doubles up as both a mixing and a serving bowl.) Cut open the little sachets and tip in all the Parmesan (weigh it if you like – you'll be astounded how little there is), half the croutons and two-thirds of the dressing. Chuck in the prawns, peas and chives. Grind in some black pepper, toss the salad thoroughly and eat.

more give the extra croutons and dressing to your partner, whose salad would also benefit from an extra ounce or two of shaved or grated Parmesan.

Instant ramen or miso soup + extra bits

Ramen may sound exotic but they are nothing more than noodles, the sort that go into Japanese-style instant soup – although they actually hail from China and well-bred Japanese people consider them very common. The soups come in lots of flavours, but many are loaded with the kind of chemicals you'd prefer to find in a tin of furniture polish. I only buy organic ramen. Then, to add a bit of verve and bulk, I bung in some fresh stuff – perhaps mushrooms, spring onions, beansprouts, ribbons of spring greens, shreds of cooked chicken or cubes of tofu. I do the same thing with plain miso soup, the delightfully cloudy, slightly sweet soup so beloved by all Japanese – whether working class or toffs. Either soup is eminently suitable for doubling up into a main course – simply throw in more ingredients.

ingredients for 1

RAMEN SOUP

1 (88g) packet of organic seaweed ramen

1 celery stick
finely sliced

1 sachet of instant miso soup powder

2–3 dashes of tamari (or Japanese soy sauce)

about 125g firm silken tofu
cut into large cubes

1 sheet of nori seaweed
toasted and cut into fine strips

(optional) a shake of furikake

Put about 600ml of cold water, the ramen noodles and celery into a large saucepan. Bring to a boil over a medium-high heat and simmer, uncovered, for 5 minutes. Whisk in the miso powder and simmer for a further 2 minutes. Add the tamari, then remove the pan from the heat and submerge the cubes of tofu in the broth. Leave for 1 minute, then serve in a deep bowl. Strew the nori and optional furikake on top just before eating.

MISO SOUP

2 sachets of instant miso soup powder

3 chestnut mushrooms
wiped clean and finely sliced

1 spring onion
trimmed and finely sliced

1 sheet of nori seaweed
toasted and cut into fine strips

Tip the miso powder into a medium saucepan and add 400ml cold water. Put the pan over a high flame and whisk to dissolve the powder while you bring the soup to a boil. Add the mushrooms and spring onion and cook for 2 minutes. Pour the soup into a bowl and strew the nori on top. Eat immediately.

Air-cured ham + fresh figs

It's hardly necessary to sing the praises of Parma ham, although San Daniele and the Spanish pata negra hams are even better. In our house plates are often redundant: the tissue-paper-thin slices of pearly pink and cream-edged ham go straight into our mouths as we peel them from the greaseproof paper. But most of us live in an imperfect world – or, at least, not next door to an Italian deli – and frequently the ham comes pre-sliced in a sealed plastic packet. While still good, it's never quite as aromatic as when the slices have just been released from a big, plump haunch. Other air-cured hams may offer a more smoky, assertive flavour. I am fond of Black Forest ham, with its venison-like hue, and Bayonne ham and speck are equally good.

Melon is an obvious partner for ham, but don't snub a juicy mango or papaya, or a well-bred ripe pear, such as Comice. But if you really want to taste heaven on a plate, serve the ham with a couple of fondant-sweet, jammy figs. The best are the tiny green Lebanese ones that are sold in punnets in September, but I also like the larger greenish mountain figs from Cyprus. As for the more usual purple figs, those from the Mediterranean area can be wonderful, but I've yet to buy any from Israel or South Africa that aren't mealy, dry and tasteless. Assuming they haven't been ruined from incarceration in cold storage, it's best to choose figs that are only slightly soft and take them home to finish ripening. When they are ready to eat, they should be bulging and heavy, with tiny beads of sugary syrup just starting to seep from the base.

ingredients for 1

a few thin slices of air-cured ham

2–3 fresh ripe figs

Arrange furls of ham on a serving plate and season with plenty of black pepper. Quickly rinse the figs, then cut a deep cross through the pointy end. Gently open up each fig into four petal-like sections and arrange the figs on the plate with the ham. I am happy to eat this particular meal with my fingers. Provided the figs are clean and ripe, and the skins are thin, you can eat them in their entirety: when the skins are thicker they are not quite so palatable.

A beefy alternative

Bresaola is Italian air-cured beef fillet. Finely sliced, it's fabulous with a sprinkling of lemon juice and some black pepper, or add a few shavings of Parmesan and a mere trickle of olive oil. A spoonful of real buffalo ricotta (not the sticky, bland commercial stuff that comes in tubs) mixed with chopped chives and parsley would also taste nice.

Gravlax + guacamole

It's quite fascinating the way food and fashion romp together: recipes and ingredients go from the unknown to the mundane in less time than it takes to clean the oven. Gravlax is a case in point. Once an esoteric Swedish novelty (although not to the Scandinavians, I hasten to add), gravlax is now as ubiquitous as smoked salmon – and has managed to lose the 'ad' from the middle of its name on the way. Guacamole, although a relative newcomer, is equally popular. But commercial success and quality do not always go hand in hand, so avoid anything that looks like green Instant Whip and head straight for the chunky fresh stuff sold in the better food stores – you know who they are. For this recipe (hardly that – it only requires a pair of scissors) you won't need the little packet of mustard sauce that usually accompanies gravlax – keep it to eat with any remaining slices or to gussy up some plain smoked fish.

ingredients for 1

3–4 tbsp chunky guacamole

a few tiny cherry tomatoes
halved

1–2 tbsp chopped spring onions or chives

a few fresh basil leaves
roughly torn

¼ lime
cut into 2 wedges

3 slices of gravlax

Scoop the guacamole into a small bowl and stir in the tomatoes, spring onion and basil leaves. Use one of the lime wedges to squeeze in a little juice – just enough to liven up the flavour.

Artfully arrange the slices of gravlax on the plate and dollop on the guacamole. Serve with the remaining wedge of lime and a couple of Krisprolls – you can pretend they are tortilla chips.

A smoky alternative
Arrange some good-quality smoked salmon, a handful of prawns and half an avocado on a plate, in whatever style takes your fancy. Season the avocado with a little salt, and everything with black pepper. Serve with a sauce made from 2 tablespoons of low-fat crème fraîche, 1 teaspoon of Dijon mustard, 1 tablespoon of chopped fresh dill and a squeeze of lemon juice to taste.

Warm chicken tikka + tzatziki salad

I can't help feeling food manufacturers are scraping the bottom of the barrel when it comes to adding new chicken lines to those already on the shelves. Chicken tikka and Chinese-style chicken are one thing but now every continent is being plundered for ideas on ways to perk up this most bland of white meats. Of course, it's only bland in the first place because they use the cheapest, battery-fed birds that haven't had a chance to develop any intrinsic flavour. An organic chicken that has been allowed to eat the sort of food chickens like to eat, as well as roam freely and live to a decent age, has abundant flavour. Anyway, chicken tikka – one of the first of the 'added-value' chicken recipes – is probably the least alarming of the lot, which is why I sometimes buy it... and then do this with it.

ingredients for 2

about 150g cooked chicken tikka fillets

3 tbsp natural low-fat yoghurt

a pinch of paprika

2 cardamom pods
crushed, husks discarded and seeds pounded

a squeeze of fresh lime juice

3 tbsp low-fat tzatziki

1 tbsp chopped fresh dill, coriander or chives

1 garlic clove
finely chopped

a few handfuls of salad leaves

Preheat the grill. Turn the chicken tikka fillets into a bowl and spoon over 2 tablespoons of natural yoghurt. Add the paprika, crushed cardamom seeds, lime juice and some black pepper, and toss thoroughly. Lay the fillets on a sturdy baking tray, then slide the tray under the grill – not too closely, or the chicken will burn before it heats through – and cook for 5–6 minutes until pasty-brown-looking. (Yoghurt does a lot for the flavour but not much for the appearance – expect the fillets to look slightly grungy.)

Meanwhile, mix the remaining yoghurt with the tzatziki, herbs and garlic, and add seasoning to taste. Arrange the salad leaves and the tikka fillets becomingly on a plate and spoon over the tzatziki.

Nice easy things to do with a bag of salad

The quality of ready-prepared salad has improved so much that I can't remember when I last bothered to compose my own selection of leaves (apart from adding in exotica from my own garden). While I will not buy any mixture which includes lollo rosso (or bianco), I snaffle up with some alacrity those that feature rocket, mizuna, little red mustard leaves, lamb's lettuce, baby spinach and watercress. For a quick lunch, I usually toss the leaves with something proteinous and add a few extra salad vegetables. I use any dressing very sparingly, remembering what's left over can be refrigerated for another day.

ingredients for 1

Toss a few handfuls of mixed leaves with a cooked chicken breast torn into pencil-thick shards; 1–2 slices of cooked tongue cut into strips; a few thickly sliced chestnut mushrooms; a small handful of chopped parsley. Dress sparingly with a vinaigrette made from 1 teaspoon of cider vinegar; a dab of Dijon mustard; seasoning; 1 tablespoon of cranberry juice; 1 tablespoon of extra-virgin olive oil.

Toss a few handfuls of wild rocket with some spring onions (or baby leeks) griddled until just tender; 2 skinless cooked chicken thighs or a duck leg, shredded into pencil-thick shards; an orange, peeled and thinly sliced; a few black (stoned) olives; ground black pepper. Dress sparingly with a vinaigrette made from 1 tablespoon of lemon juice; seasoning; 3 tablespoons of extra-virgin olive oil.

Toss a few handfuls of trimmed watercress with a head of Belgian chicory, separated; 3 strips of cooked streaky bacon, crumbled; a few chopped chives or 1 spring onion; a handful of fresh (or defrosted frozen) cockles. Dress very sparingly with a vinaigrette made from 1 tablespoon of grain mustard; a pinch of caster sugar; seasoning; 1 teaspoon of tarragon vinegar; 2 tablespoons of groundnut oil; a dash of single cream.

Toss a few handfuls of Little Gem or torn Cos with a handful of halved cherry tomatoes; a handful of lightly cooked French beans; a few strips of anchovy; a half-dozen black olives; a small can of tuna, well drained; a softish hard-boiled egg, peeled and quartered. Dress lightly with a vinaigrette made from 1 tablespoon of red wine vinegar; a dab of mustard; seasoning; 3 tablespoons of extra-virgin olive oil.

Toss a few handfuls of ruby chard and beetroot-based salad (aka bistro salad) with a handful of raw peas; 2–3 slices of pastrami cut into thin strips; half a peeled avocado cut into chunks. Dress sparingly with a vinaigrette made from 1 teaspoon of creamed horseradish; 1 teaspoon of white wine vinegar; seasoning; 2 tablespoons of groundnut oil.

EATING with your DARLING

I am as happy eating junk as the next person. What I cannot stand is pretentious food that's sourced from poor materials and then tricked up to be something it isn't. Back in the Eighties we suffered nouvelle cuisine as interpreted by a barrage of dimwitted chefs and now we're being bombarded from every quarter with so-called fusion food. In the hands of an intelligent exponent, such as Peter Gordon, this style of eclectic cooking can be fantastic. Unfortunately, most chefs seem to think that all it involves is cramming a myriad contradictory ingredients together. There is no appreciation of harmony, relevance or cultural background.

I am quite aware that to many people the recipes in this book may appear equally hifalutin and inaccessible. They aren't. Firstly, the food may frequently be of Asian rather than European origin but within that context the flavours will be traditional and interdependent. You will not find chicken and tamarillo risotto with sauerkraut ciabatta, or any other disparate nonsense. Perhaps more importantly, the vast majority of ingredients can be found in any mainstream supermarket. Unlike many cookery writers, I live deep in the countryside and, with the exception of a good local farm shop and butcher's, most of our food comes from a supermarket 30 miles away. I also use the web, which is seething with enthusiastic mail-order firms prepared to send out the most rarefied ingredients.

Asian or otherwise, the preponderance of assertive, whip-lashing flavours in my recipes is entirely deliberate. Anyone who has attempted to lose weight on a regime of lettuce and cottage cheese, with the odd chicken breast thrown in for light relief, will know how quickly one runs out of enthusiasm for dietary food and its inherent blandness. In fact, I happen to be rather fond of wimpish foods like tofu, but when I am having a difficult day and struggling a little, then it's savoury, saliva-inducing flavours that I crave.

A few years ago I found out that the four basic tastes – salty, bitter, sour and sweet – had been joined by a fifth, called umami, from the Japanese word for deliciousness (*sic*). That was all I knew until I opened Jeffrey Steingarten's riveting book, *It Must Be Something I Ate*. There I read about the discovery, in 1908, that the active taste ingredient in giant kelp (the seaweed which provides the pivotal flavour for the ubiquitous Japanese stock called dashi) is glutamic acid. In the human body, this is the most common amino acid and it links up with other amino acids to form various proteins. However, in its separate form glutamic acid 'lends food a richly savoury taste, a perception of thickness and "mouthfulness"' and this is umami.

To the many scientists who believe in the concept of discrete basic tastes, umami qualifies on the grounds that it stimulates a separate set of nerves and receptors in the mouth – quite independently of the other four basic tastes.

Two other umami substances have since been discovered, inosinate and guanylate, found in bonito (tuna) and shiitake (mushrooms) respectively. But what's more thrilling – to me – is that while giant kelp has the highest concentration of glutamic acid, the food with the second highest level is... wait for it... Parmesan. Frankly, I think this is brilliant news and surely explains why even a light dusting of this powerfully flavoured cheese improves so many dishes, Italian or otherwise. (And, yes, I know it should be called Parmigiano Reggiano but when Italian footballers stop diving, I'll start using the correct Italian.) Following right behind Parmesan comes tomato paste, which also makes complete sense when you think how many people are unable to eat their chips without a bright-red flood of ketchup. How it works is that the large quantity of free glutamate in Parmesan and tomato paste acts synergistically when it comes into contact with the smaller levels of umami present in other foods and greatly intensifies the flavour. It's rather marvellous to discover that there is some genuine physiological reason for why I am so in thrall to ingredients such as shiitake and crab. And, to add to my wonder and bafflement, I also discovered that free glutamate is the naturally occurring form of MSG – which gives cause to question how people complain of headaches induced by Chinese restaurant food, but you rarely hear anyone blaming Italian pizzas for causing a migraine.

Science and flavour aside, it will have become apparent that the *Fat Girl Slim* diet is not for everyone. In the same spirit of honesty that allows you to share in my failures, my foibles and my fat, I acknowledge that no one who is short of a bob or two and has a young family (probably the reason for the former) could begin to follow the principles of my diet. Apart from the expense, the style of cooking is unlikely to appeal to anyone other than an adult with a reasonably sophisticated palate or, at least, a willingness to try unfamiliar foods, the latter a trait not normally associated with children. Being childless is a great regret but there is a tiny consolation in knowing that I have only my husband and myself to please and if I want to eat exotically and/or healthily I can. I simply don't know how any woman can go on a successful diet when she's surrounded by young children demanding a relentless stream of junk food. It may not cause physical scars watching other people scoff a stack of hot gold-glistened French fries but the mental anguish is acute. My only (unhelpful) advice is to leave home for a few months.

For those without children or financial worries, I am unrepentant in my belief that one should be prepared to pay what it costs for good food. To me, eating well matters. Compared with other European countries, we are notorious for having the lowest spend *per capita* on food: apparently, we would far rather splash out on holidays and clothes than properly matured cheese or naturally leavened bread. Personally, I see no reason why milk, eggs or chicken should be dirt-cheap, but our history is one of early industrialisation and the concept of low-cost, mass-produced, processed food is endemic. Fortunately, my husband is equally happy about squandering our hard-earned money on food (and wine) and, to a large extent, shares my diet – or it wouldn't work. It also helps that, while not fat, he is not exactly svelte.

One of the tricks I use to make sure both of us are satisfied with our intake is to bulk out David's meal with extra fat or carbohydrate – or both. In simple terms, this may mean he gets potatoes, rice or pasta while I don't.

Occasionally, it's not extra calories that are required for him, but less for me. Caesar salad is a good example: I skimp on the Parmesan, dressing and croutons, and give the excess to him. And, if supper is a bowl of chunky vegetable soup, I'll make David a couple of slices of Welsh Rabbit to eat on the side, while I look on plaintively – and have another bowl of soup. Where appropriate, you'll find this clip-on/clip-off concept flagged up at the end of the recipe.

It will also be fairly obvious that most of the recipes in this chapter are geared towards an evening meal. I suppose there are some couples who stay at home all day and have lunch together but, generally, they are retired. I don't think this book will have much appeal for such people, nor should it. If I get to be a septuagenarian, I hope I won't give a fig about what I look like (apart from being clean) or what I eat. I may even take up smoking. After a lifetime of weight-watching there has to be a point when you can let it all hang out, both figuratively and literally. To return to the point, I have always regarded supper or dinner as a celebratory meal to mark the end of a long hard day. The diktat that says no one should eat later than 6.00 pm was obviously dreamt up before the days when women went out to work – and our entire transport system ground to a halt. As a restaurateur, I seldom leave work before 10.00 pm, but nowadays even teachers are lucky if they get home in time for *Coronation Street*. I can see that having a huge supper prior to bedtime is probably not ideal but I am rather relieved that, in a weight-losing context, recent research indicates that it matters not a jot when you eat.

What does matter is bringing some sense of style to your meal. This is important at the best of times but when you are dieting it is crucial. Slapping a low-fat lasagne on a dingy plate and downing it in front of the television is not going to make you feel good about anything, least of all the limited number of calories you are allowed to hoover up. You must pay attention to the trappings if you are going to feel like a grown-up with free choice rather than a recalcitrant child about to be sent to bed without supper. So, take some time to choose serving dishes or plates that complement the food – go out and buy a few Asian-style bowls, chopsticks and little dipping bowls, if necessary. Use decent cutlery, glassware and proper linen or cotton napkins, rather than skimpy paper serviettes. (Don't even think about polyester napkins unless you run a third-rate steak joint in Barnet and believe deep-dyed burgundy napery is quite the thing.) Treat yourself to an elegantly designed bottle of sparkling (or still) water even though it is outrageously priced and no healthier than tap water: it will be some consolation for not drinking (much, or any) wine. Bother to garnish the food, not spuriously, but with appropriate flavoursome herbs, seeds, salad leaves or wedges of citrus fruit. Above all, eat your meal at a properly set table and try to extend it over at least two courses, if not three: the third need only be a starter comprising one slice of smoked salmon or a dessert of strawberries lightly spiced with ground black pepper. It may all sound sickeningly Martha Stewart-ish, but I promise it's worth making an effort. Feeling you have dined like a queen rather than an overweight frump is as much to do with psychology as reality.

Last but not least, none of the recipes that follow should take longer than 45 minutes to put together and many are much faster than that. I know only too well how infuriating it is to come home after a hard day's work, itching with hunger and tiredness, and then have to cook. With a quick-but-damaging cheese and pickle sandwich only a breadboard away, it is vital that it should only take a little more time to put something filling but not fattening on the table.

Smoked haddock + poached egg

Smoked haddock for breakfast is a bit too stomach-heaving for my sensibilities, so it's only at supper that this quintessentially British dish puts in an appearance at our house. As with anything simple, the quality of the ingredients is ruthlessly exposed, so buy undyed smoked haddock and organic (or at least free-range) eggs – the latter must be spanking-fresh or they won't hold their shape.

(Poached eggs can be held for up to 24 hours in the fridge, submerged in clean cold water: before serving, drain off the cold water and replace it with a kettleful of boiling water. Leave the eggs for 1 minute to warm through, then drain them thoroughly on a pad of kitchen paper before serving.)

ingredients for 2

2–3 large eggs (see note above)

2 (175g each) smoked haddock fillets
trimmed of any hard or thin flappy bits

Bring a few inches of water to a strong simmer in a large, shallow pan. Break the eggs into the water in a neat, controlled action, using a spoon to help furl the whites around the yolks. Poach for 2–3 minutes, or until the whites are set but the yolks are still soft – you'll see them wobbling around underneath the filmy top layer. Lift the eggs out with a slotted spoon and scissor off any scruffy edges. If using them immediately, keep the eggs warm.

Rinse out the pan, fill it with a scant inch of water and bring it to a gentle simmer over a low-medium flame. Put in the smoked haddock, skin-side down. Cover the pan and poach the fish for about 5 minutes or until the flesh is just opaque. Drain the haddock then remove and discard the dark skin. Put the fish on two warmed plates, place the eggs on top and season generously with black pepper – you shouldn't need any salt. Serve immediately.

more darling can have 2 eggs and a slice of buttered bread underneath the haddock. A few rashers of grilled dry-cured bacon would not go amiss either.
less eat in the other room – the smell of bacon and the stack of bread may prove too tempting.

Aubergine 'lasagne'

A traducement of a classic dish, in this recipe I have replaced the layers of pasta traditionally found in a lasagne with layers of aubergine. Ah well, it still tastes very good. What's more, this is one of those nice patient dishes that can be made up to 48 hours ahead and then reheated in a moderate oven.

ingredients for 2

3 aubergines
sliced fairly thinly lengthways

2 tbsp olive oil

2 medium carrots
peeled and finely chopped

2 celery sticks
finely chopped

3 garlic cloves
crushed and finely chopped

8 chestnut mushrooms
wiped clean and finely chopped

a few sprigs of fresh marjoram and/or thyme and/or basil
leaves only (tear the basil roughly)

2 pinches of mild paprika

500g tomato passata

1 (400g) can of Italian plum tomatoes
just the tomatoes, yellowy-green stems discarded and flesh roughly chopped

1 (50g) can of anchovies
the fillets drained and split lengthways

Bring a very large saucepan of water to the boil and blanch the aubergine slices for 1 minute: do this in batches and make sure the water remains on the boil. Drain and pat the slices dry with kitchen paper.

Preheat the oven to 170°C fan/gas mark 5. Heat a large sauté (or deep frying) pan over a low-medium heat and then add the oil. Tip in the carrots, celery, garlic and mushrooms, and stir thoroughly. Cook the vegetables gently for about 10 minutes, or until they look wilted. Stir in the herbs, paprika, passata, tomatoes and plenty of seasoning, then continue to cook for a further 10 minutes, or until the sauce is pretty well homogenised.

Line the bottom of a large, deep ovenproof dish with a layer of aubergine then strew on a few strips of anchovy. Cover with a layer of the sauce. Repeat until all the aubergines and sauce have been used up, finishing with a thin layer of sauce. Bake the 'lasagne' in the oven for 25–30 minutes, or until hot and bubbling.

more grate a lavish amount of Parmesan over your darling's portion.

Griddled scallops + tomato and ginger sauce

I adore scallops: the dense but tender flesh and rich, sweetish flavour are unlike anything else. But it's really important to buy fresh scallops, even though they are expensive. (And beware of the very white scallops that unscrupulous fishmongers have deliberately soaked in water to increase the size.) Even if the scallops have already been shucked, you will still need to remove the fine elastic tissue and small thick whitish pad that secures the coral to the pearly-white nugget of flesh. This is a simple yet delightful recipe.

ingredients for 2

a dash of olive oil, plus a drop more

2 garlic cloves
crushed and finely chopped

½ mild red chilli
de-seeded and finely chopped

a pinch of ground cinnamon

3–4 vine tomatoes (depending on size)
blanched, skinned, cored, de-seeded
and roughly chopped

1 small 'thumb' of root ginger
peeled and grated

a handful of parsley
leaves roughly chopped

**6 thin slices of pancetta
(or streaky bacon)**

10 large scallops
trimmed, rinsed and patted dry with
kitchen paper

(to serve) a handful of wild rocket

Heat a large non-stick frying pan over a low flame. Add a dash of oil and throw in the garlic and chilli. Fry gently for 2 minutes, stirring occasionally, then stir in the cinnamon and cook for 30 seconds. Add the tomatoes, ginger and some seasoning, raise the heat and cook for 2–3 minutes, stirring frequently. Add the parsley and cook for a further 1–2 minutes, or until the sauce is soft and sludgy. Keep the sauce warm.

Meanwhile, grill the pancetta until it is crisp. Drain the slices on kitchen paper and keep them warm.

Heat a heavy frying pan over a medium-high flame for 2–3 minutes. Lightly oil and season the scallops, then cook them for 2–3 minutes, undisturbed. Turn and continue cooking for another 1–2 minutes, or until the scallops are caramelised on the outside and barely opaque inside.

Puddle some sauce in the middle of each plate and surround it with the scallops. Pile a little bundle of rocket in the middle and perch the pancetta slices on top. Or do your own thing – it's allowed.

Grilled sardines + lemon and garlic couscous stuffing

Sardines have a stunning flavour and are so cheap it's ridiculous. The only possible reason for their being so under-rated is because people do not like having to fiddle around with the little bones. So, fillet the sardines first – it won't take more than 15 minutes. Of course, you can eat the sardines plainly grilled, but I like my way of stuffing them with flavoured couscous. Sardines vary hugely in size, often looking as big as herrings – hence the latitude in the quantity required.

ingredients for 2

4–8 sardines (depending on size)

1 (110g) box of flavoured part-prepared couscous

a pinch of Marigold Swiss vegetable bouillon powder

a little extra-virgin olive oil

a few sprigs of parsley
finely chopped

1 lemon
cut into wedges

a bundle of interesting salad leaves

(optional) slices of toasted ciabatta and/or a little pesto

Cut the heads off the sardines, then slit open the bellies and scrape out the innards. Give the sardines a quick rinse and pat them dry. Place a sardine on the work surface, belly down and with the opening splayed out, and press down firmly along the backbone. Using scissors, sever the spine at the tail-end, then gently pull it out, starting at the head-end: it will lift out effortlessly, taking most of the hair-fine bones with it. Do the same with the remaining sardines, then slash each one 3 times on one side only.

Make up the couscous following the instructions on the packet but add a pinch of stock powder to the water and use a little olive oil rather than the suggested vegetable oil. Stir in the parsley when the couscous is ready and leave it to cool.

Preheat the grill. Line the grill pan with foil and lightly oil it. Stuff a good wodge of couscous into each sardine, as well as in the slashes, then lay the sardines in the pan. Use a lemon wedge to sprinkle over some juice, then season. Grill the little fishes – not too close to the elements – for 5–8 minutes, or until they are golden and crisp. Serve them on warmed plates with lemon wedges and some salad.

more drizzle the ciabatta with a little olive oil or a smearing of pesto and place the non-dieter's sardines on top.

Salmon teriyaki + wilted greens

Salmon and tuna are often served quite rare nowadays, but I'd far rather my fish was either completely raw, as in sashimi, or just-cooked in the middle, as in the recipe below. The combination of sweetly lacquered fish and lively stir-fried greens is fashionable but none the worse for that. Cook the salmon and wilted greens simultaneously in two separate pans.

ingredients for 2

2 (175g) salmon escalopes
the skin de-scaled but left on

**2 tbsp sake
(or very dry sherry)**

1 tsp caster sugar

2 tbsp soy sauce

2 tbsp mirin

1 small 'thumb' of root ginger
peeled and grated

a little groundnut (or vegetable) oil, plus 1 tbsp

3 spring onions
trimmed and cut in thirds
at an angle

1 garlic clove
crushed and finely chopped

3 pak choi
separated into leaves,
root-ends trimmed

100g beansprouts
any discoloured sprouts
discarded

Put the salmon in a close-fitting, non-reactive dish. Whisk the sake, sugar, soy sauce, mirin and ginger together, and pour over the fish. Leave the escalopes to marinate in the fridge for at least 30 minutes, preferably 2 hours. Drain the marinade into a small saucepan and bring to a boil over a high heat, uncovered. Continue to boil for just 2 minutes, or until the marinade is a tad thicker. Set the pan aside.

Pat the salmon dry with kitchen paper and very lightly oil the escalopes on both sides. Place a heavy frying pan over a medium-high flame and, when it is very hot, put in the salmon, skin-side down. Cook for 4 minutes, brushing the salmon with the marinade halfway through. Turn the fish and baste again. Cook for 4–6 minutes, depending on the thickness, again basting. The salmon is ready when it has just turned from translucent to opaque in the middle.

Meanwhile, heat the remaining oil in a wok or large frying pan over a medium flame. Toss in the spring onions, garlic and pak choi, and stir-fry for a few minutes until wilted. Add the beansprouts, toss thoroughly and pour in a dash of the marinade. Continue to stir-fry for 1–2 minutes, or until the veg is tender-crisp, then divide it between 2 plates. Perch the salmon on top, skin-side up, and brush over any remaining marinade. (Please eat the skin – it's almost the best part.)

Spice-rubbed cod + vegetables

As I write, there's a real probability that there will be a total fishing ban on cod (and many other of our traditional North Atlantic fishes). It's all down to the big 'factory' boats which have wreaked havoc on traditional, nature-respecting fishing traditions. My advice is to enjoy this simple, flavour-saturated dish while you can. Oh, and although this recipe looks very long-winded it only takes about 30 minutes, marinating time aside.

ingredients for 2

I scant tsp each of ground cumin, paprika piccante (or a pinch of chilli and a scant tsp paprika), turmeric and dried oregano

3 garlic cloves
crushed and finely chopped

2 (175g) cod fillets
skin left on

a little olive oil, plus I tbsp

I red onion
cut into eighths with root attached

I fennel bulb
trimmed and cut as the onion

I large courgette
cut at an angle into thick slices

a pinch of saffron threads

250ml vegetable or fish stock

2 (canned) piquillo peppers
cut into thick strips

a small handful of fresh coriander
leaves roughly chopped

Combine the spices, oregano and two-thirds of the garlic on a flat plate. Smear the cod with a little oil, season, then press both sides into the spice mixture. Leave the cod to marinate for at least I hour, preferably 2.

In a large amount of boiling water, successively blanch the onion for I minute, the fennel for I minute and the courgette for 30 seconds. Refresh each veg in ice-cold water, then blot them completely dry with kitchen paper.

Heat the remaining oil in a shallow saucepan over a medium flame. Fry the remaining garlic and the onion for 2 minutes, then add the saffron and fry for 30 seconds. Add the fennel and stock, bring to a simmer and cook for 3 minutes. Add the courgette, carry on cooking for about 3 minutes, then put in the piquillo peppers and coriander just to warm them through.

Meanwhile, heat a heavy non-stick frying pan over a medium-high flame. Put in the cod skin-side down, and cook, undisturbed, for 3 minutes. Turn the fillets carefully, reduce the heat and continue to cook for 6–8 minutes, or until the flesh is just opaque. Divide the veg and broth between two bowls and put the cod on top.

more a dollop of rouille or aïoli on the cod would be nice.

Warm chicken liver and grape salad

Chicken livers are wonderfully versatile, but I particularly like them in a warm salad with bitter leaves. Here the livers are cooked with toasted spices and nutty-flavoured garlic, and juicy grapes provide a pleasing sweet-but-spiky foil to the rich crumbly livers.

ingredients for 2

1 tbsp olive oil

a scrap of unsalted butter

2 garlic cloves
finely sliced

a good pinch each of ground cumin, ground coriander and ground cinnamon

about 250g chicken livers (fresh, if possible)
trimmed of all threads and greenish bits

3 tbsp rice (or cider) vinegar

1 small 'thumb' of root ginger
peeled and grated

a handful of small seedless grapes

a small handful of fresh coriander
leaves chopped

a few handfuls of watercress, baby spinach and rocket

Place a largish non-stick frying pan over a medium-high flame. Add the olive oil and butter and, when the fat stops sizzling, throw in the garlic. Cook it for 1–2 minutes until barely coloured, stirring almost constantly. Still stirring, add the spices and fry them for 1 minute.

Reduce the heat to medium, season the chicken livers and throw them in the pan. Cook the livers for 2–3 minutes, tossing them frequently, until they are crusty outside but still pink in the middle. Scoop them out and keep them warm. Add the vinegar and ginger to the pan and bring to a boil, scraping up all the bits with a wooden spoon. Add the grapes and cook them for 1 minute. Put back the livers and gently stir until everything is piping hot, then stir in the coriander.

Divide the leaves between 2 serving plates, then spoon over the contents of the pan. Eat immediately.

more in a separate pan, sauté some cooked sliced new potatoes in olive oil and butter, and toss them with the livers. Or, add some largish croutons to the salad leaves, which could also be dressed in a simple vinaigrette.
less treat yourself to more grapes or add some raw, sliced chestnut mushrooms to the salad leaves.

Calves' liver + sweet and sour courgettes

If you've only eaten pigs' liver and couldn't stand either the taste or the texture, I have every sympathy. It's revolting. In contrast, calves' liver is tender, mild-flavoured – and expensive. Here, the combination of sweet onions, snazzy mint and limpid courgettes goes well with the gentle earthiness of the liver.

ingredients for 2

200g courgettes
topped, tailed and sliced into fine rounds, then spread out and salted

1 tbsp olive oil

1 onion
chopped into small dice

2 garlic cloves
crushed and finely chopped

1 tbsp white wine vinegar

1 scant tsp caster sugar

6–8 fresh mint leaves
bundled up and finely sliced

FOR THE LIVER

1 tbsp olive oil

about 225g calves' liver
trimmed and cut into fine, thin strips

3 tbsp red wine

a small handful of parsley
leaves finely chopped

Rinse the courgettes and pat the slices dry with kitchen paper. Put the olive oil into a large non-stick frying pan and heat it over a low flame. Tip in the onion and garlic and gently fry for about 15 minutes, stirring frequently. Remove the onion and garlic to a dish, draining any fat back into the pan. Turn up the heat, add the courgettes and fry for 3–5 minutes, stirring frequently, until the courgettes are tender and light golden. Season, then stir in the vinegar, sugar and mint, and cook for 3–4 minutes. Put back the onion and garlic, and set the pan aside.

Heat a large non-stick frying pan over a medium-high flame, then add the olive oil. Season the liver and add it to the pan when the oil is very hot. Cook for about 2 minutes, tossing the strips constantly, until brown but still blushed with pink in the middle. Scoop the liver out and add to the courgette mixture.

Replace the unwashed pan over a high heat and pour in the wine. Bubble it furiously, scraping up any bits, then tip the liver mixture back in and add the parsley. Stir for 1–2 minutes, until piping hot, then serve immediately.

more buy some ready-made polenta, the sort that comes in a plastic-wrapped block. Cut 2 or 3 slices, about 1 centimetre thick, paint with olive oil and grill each side until browned.

Yoghurt-marinated chicken + spiced green lentils

For me, lentils are up there with Maltesers, lobster, bacon sandwiches and sashimi – well, at least 50 per cent of that list isn't fattening. As lentils keep very happily in the fridge and take no exception to being heated up, I've allowed for plenty of leftovers. (Lentil salad with soft-boiled eggs and tapenade is fabulous.) The chicken could easily be replaced by grilled lamb or fish: like Player's, it's the lentils that count.

ingredients for 2

3 tbsp natural yoghurt

1 garlic clove
crushed and finely chopped

a good pinch each of ground cumin and ground coriander

a small pinch each of turmeric and chilli powder

2 organic chicken breasts
skin removed (sadly)

a little olive oil

FOR THE LENTILS

1 tbsp olive oil

1 large red onion
finely chopped

2 garlic cloves
crushed and finely chopped

1 small mild red chilli
de-seeded and finely chopped

2 pinches of turmeric

1 small cinnamon stick

1 star anise

4 green cardamom pods
bashed, husks discarded and seeds crushed

175g Puy or Umbrian lentils
well rinsed

700ml hot chicken or vegetable stock

2 medium tomatoes
skinned, de-seeded and roughly chopped

a large handful of coriander and/or parsley
leaves roughly chopped

Mix the yoghurt, garlic and spices into a thick paste. Slash each chicken breast a few times, then massage in the paste. Leave the breasts to marinate in the fridge for 2 to 6 hours.

For the lentils, heat the olive oil in a large heavy pan over a low-medium flame. Tip in the onion, garlic and chilli, and stir thoroughly. Cook gently for 10–15 minutes, stirring occasionally, until the onions have softened. Add the spices and fry for 1–2 minutes, stirring. Raise the heat, add the lentils and stock, and bring to a boil, uncovered. Reduce to a steady simmer and cook for 15–20 minutes, adding a good pinch of salt towards the end.

When the lentils are barely resilient to the bite, remove the pan from the heat. Season them with black pepper, add more salt if necessary, then stir in the tomatoes and herbs, and cook for 2–3 more minutes – they should be a sloppy, sauce-like mass. Keep the lentils warm if you are using them straight away.

To cook the chicken, place a non-stick frying pan over a medium flame and, when it is hot, add a drop of olive oil. Scrape off any excess marinade from the chicken, then fry the breasts for 4 minutes without disturbing them. Turn the breasts, lower the heat and continue to fry for 6–8 minutes, or until the chicken is nice and crusty-looking, and the flesh is cooked but juicy.

Remove (and discard) the cinnamon stick and star anise, then spoon the lentils on to the plates and put the chicken on top.

more pak choi, quickly stir-fried with a little sesame oil, goes very well with spicy dishes and lentils in particular. Don't overcook it, though, as soggy pak choi is truly disgusting.
less you can have some pak choi, too – but go easy on the sesame oil.

Lindsey B's warm chicken & runner bean salad

My admiration for Lindsey Bareham, who has written a daily recipe for the London *Evening Standard* since time immemorial, knows no bounds. How she manages to summon up the enthusiasm, never mind the energy, to put together a daily cookery column, I'll never know. This highly seasonal recipe – only English runner beans will do – is typical of her love of honest, simple food. I've kept to her suggestion for cutting the runner beans shoestring-style because they look so pretty in this salad, although normally I favour long diamond shapes.

ingredients for 2

5 boneless chicken thighs

about 200g runner beans
topped and tailed, strung and sliced shoestring-style

2 handfuls of cherry tomatoes
halved

8–12 fresh mint leaves
bundled up and finely sliced

a pencil-thick bundle of fresh chives
chopped

(optional) 1 tbsp chopped fresh dill

1 tbsp fresh lime juice

3 tbsp extra-virgin olive oil

Preheat the oven to 220°C fan/gas mark 8. Season the chicken thighs, then put them in a sturdy roasting tin and cook them for 35–40 minutes, or until the skin is crisp and crackling. (If using bone-in thighs, cook them for about 50 minutes.) Pull the chicken into thick shards as soon as it is cool enough to handle. (See below for what to do about the skin.)

After the chicken has been in the oven for about 25 minutes, bring a large saucepan of salted water to a boil over a high flame, then throw in the beans. Cook them, uncovered, for 2–3 minutes after the the water has returned to the boil – they should be just tender. Drain the beans thoroughly.

Tip the beans into a large warmed bowl and add the chicken, tomatoes and herbs. Whisk the lime juice and oil together, pour it into the bowl and toss the salad thoroughly. Serve while still warm.

more serve the salad panzanella-style, by tossing in small rags of torn stale ciabatta or Pugliese bread. Slim but greedy partners can also eat the crisp chicken skin, cut into thin strips.
less do not eat the skin!

The best lamb burgers

This recipe started out life as staff supper at our hotel, the Crown and Castle, it being an efficient, cost-effective way of using up the trimmings from the rumps of lamb that are a regular feature on the hotel's Trinity bistro menu. They taste so good we sometimes serve them to guests: oddly enough, it takes the more sophisticated punters to recognise that this poor man's satellite dish is actually more ravishing than the mother ship. And how we've gotten into *Star Wars* mode is quite a puzzle.

ingredients for 2

1 small 'thumb' of root ginger
peeled and grated

2 garlic cloves
crushed and finely chopped

1 shallot
finely chopped

1 mild red chilli
de-seeded and finely chopped

2–3 pinches of ground cumin

4 green cardamom pods
bashed, husks discarded and seeds finely crushed

a good pinch of ground coriander

a good pinch of allspice

a small handful of fresh coriander
leaves finely chopped

2 tbsp low-fat natural yoghurt

about 400g coarsely minced lean lamb

1 small egg white
whisked

a little olive oil

Combine everything, except the lamb, egg white and oil, in a large bowl. Season with plenty of pepper (not salt), then tip in the minced lamb and the egg white. Mix everything together lightly but thoroughly, then form the mixture into 4 plump patties. Try not to compress the meat as it will make the burgers tough. Refrigerate them for 30 minutes. (No longer, as the acidity of the yoghurt breaks down the meat and makes the texture too smooth.)

Heat a heavy non-stick frying pan over a medium-high flame. Very lightly oil the burgers, then season them with salt. When the pan is really hot, put in the burgers and cook them, undisturbed, for 3 minutes. Turn and cook them for a further 5–6 minutes, or until just pink in the middle. Leave them for a few minutes before serving.

more serve the burgers on toasted ciabatta with a dollop of Greek yoghurt enlivened with chopped mint, parsley or coriander. Or, high-roast a mélange of root vegetables, dusted with spices and tossed in olive oil, for 30–40 minutes.

less have a spoonful of low-fat natural yoghurt mixed with herbs and a Greek-style salad, minus the feta.

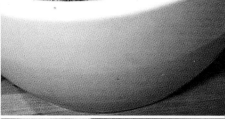

One-pan pork and peppers

There is absolutely nothing remarkable about this Chinese-style stir-fry, but it's easy, filling and zippy. As with all recipes of this ilk, it is essential to have everything ready before the (very quick) cooking commences.

ingredients for 2

1 tsp cornflour

2 tbsp dark soy sauce

2 tbsp dry sherry

1 tbsp groundnut (or vegetable) oil

about 200g pork fillet (tenderloin)
trimmed and cut into small bite-sized chunks

2 large (or 1 banana) shallot(s)
cut into medium dice

2 garlic cloves
crushed and finely chopped

1 small red pepper
de-seeded and cut into medium dice

1 small 'thumb' of root ginger
peeled and grated

2 handfuls of beansprouts

2 spring onions
trimmed and roughly sliced

Whisk the cornflour, soy sauce and sherry together to make a smooth paste. Leave to one side.

Put a large non-stick wok (or huge frying pan) over a medium-high flame and, when it is hot, add the oil. Swish the oil around to coat the wok, then tip out any excess. Quickly throw in the chunks of pork and fry them for 5–6 minutes, tossing and stirring almost constantly, until the meat is golden and cooked.

Add the shallot(s), garlic, red pepper and ginger, and fry for about 3 minutes, tossing constantly. Stir in the beansprouts and cook them for 1 minute. Pour the cornflour mixture into the wok, together with 100ml water, and bring to a boil. Add the spring onions, stir once again, then serve immediately in deep bowls.

more serve less's portion first, then stir 1 tablespoon of toasted peanuts or cashews into the remainder. You could also heat up a packet of egg-fried rice. (Or, heaven forbid, make some: put a portion of cooked basmati rice into a large frying pan and stir in 1 small beaten egg, a few dashes of soy, 1 chopped spring onion and 1 tablespoon of sesame oil. Move everything around for 2 minutes, then serve.)
less as you were.

Lamb chops + garlic and spinach pilaf

Although I am quite fond of loin chops, charred on the outside and pink in the middle, I'm baffled by the huge appeal lamb has for most people. It wouldn't bother me if I never ate it again. Here, the pilaf is the star – the chops are only there for hubby's sake.

ingredients for 2

1 tbsp olive oil, plus a smidgen

1 tsp each of ground cumin and ground coriander

a pinch of hot chilli powder

225g basmati rice
very well rinsed and drained

450ml chicken or vegetable stock

1 whole head of garlic
split into separate cloves, then blanched and peeled

1 bay leaf (fresh or dried)

3 medium tomatoes
de-seeded and roughly chopped

225g young leaf spinach
trimmed, rinsed and drained

a handful of parsley
leaves chopped

**4–6 loin chops
(depending on greed)**

Heat 1 tablespoon of oil in a large, wide non-stick pan over a low-medium flame. When it is hot, add the spices and fry them for 1 minute, stirring constantly, then add the rice. Pour in the stock, stir and add the garlic, bay leaf, tomatoes and seasoning. Cover the pan, raise the heat and bring the contents to a boil. Stir, then reduce the heat and slowly simmer the rice, covered, for 13–15 minutes.

Meanwhile, heat a large wok over a medium flame, then pile in the still-damp spinach and some salt. Cook until the leaves begin to wilt, tossing them constantly with tongs or salad servers.

When the rice is just tender and looks pretty dry, stir in the spinach and parsley. Remove the pan from the heat and place a folded tea towel under the lid. Leave the pilaf to rest for 10 minutes in a warm place, then fluff it up with a fork just before serving.

Meanwhile, heat a griddle over a medium-high flame. Oil the lamb chops very skimpily, then season them. When the griddle is smoking hot, put in the chops and leave them, undisturbed, for 3 minutes. Reduce the heat, turn the chops and cook them for a further 4–8 minutes, depending on thickness and how pink you like your meat.

more lamb and pilaf are both suckers for a splurge of tzatziki or thick Greek yoghurt.

Tofu, shiitake and coriander broth

My Asian-style broths are mostly variations on a theme but it's remarkable how different they taste from each other, depending on the vegetables employed and the seasonings. Which type of noodle or rice that goes in also makes a difference, well at least enough for me to remain interested – and you, hopefully.

ingredients for 2

2 tbsp Marigold Swiss vegetable bouillon powder

2 garlic cloves
crushed and finely chopped

2 medium carrots
peeled and cut into medium dice

1 large leek
pale green and white part only,
cut into small bite-sized chunks

1 'thumb' of root ginger
peeled and grated

125g fine egg noodles

8 fresh shiitake mushrooms
the caps slashed with a cross

a small bunch of fresh coriander
leaves roughly chopped

1 (250g) box of firm silken tofu
cut into 8–10 large cubes

(optional) Japanese pepper

Put the Marigold powder, 1.7 litres of cold water, the garlic, carrots, leek and ginger into a very large saucepan or wok and bring to a boil. Reduce the heat and simmer strongly for about 10 minutes, or until the vegetables are nearly cooked.

Throw in the noodles and shiitake, season, then continue to simmer for 2–3 minutes, or until the noodles are just tender. Stir in the coriander, then carefully plop in the cubes of tofu, making sure they are covered with the broth. Turn off the heat and leave for 2–3 minutes to allow the tofu to heat through thoroughly – it doesn't need cooking as such. Divide the broth between 2 large bowls, season with optional Japanese pepper and serve immediately.

more cook a whole (250g) packet of noodles and have three-quarters of them.

Green onion soup

Traditional French onion soup can be glorious – it can also be a muddy, insipid cesspit of dull-tasting broth, claggy cheese and sloppy bread. I decided to make a version that was invigorated by fresh green onions and herbs rather than deadened with a slump of grease and starch. Jolly good it is, too. I always make soup in quantity, so there's plenty here for another day.

ingredients for 2+

1 tbsp olive oil

30g unsalted butter

5 garlic cloves
crushed and chopped

3 large Spanish onions
chopped roughly into medium dice

3 tbsp brandy

1.5 litres hot water

2 tbsp Swiss Marigold vegetable bouillon powder

1 bunch of spring onions
trimmed and chopped

a large handful of parsley
roughly chopped

Heat the olive oil and butter in a very large saucepan over a low flame, then tip in the garlic and onions. Stir thoroughly, then cook very gently, uncovered and stirring occasionally, for about 40 minutes. At the end of this time the onions should be soft, silky and pale gold: if they start browning too quickly, then reduce the heat.

Turn up the heat to medium-high and cook the onions for a further 10–12 minutes, stirring them almost constantly, until they are a deeper gold. Add the brandy – it should bubble and disappear almost immediately. Add the hot water, stock powder and plenty of seasoning. Stir thoroughly, scraping up any residue from the bottom of the pan so the broth is nicely coloured. Simmer the soup for 25 minutes, half-covered, then throw in the spring onions and parsley, and simmer for a further 5 minutes.

more despite my introductory comments, you could toast a day-old slice of ciabatta, load it with grated Gruyère and float it on the soup. You could also put the bowl under the grill so the cheese bubbles and browns. Personally, I would prefer to eat some toasted cheese on the side, but being the dieter… **less**… the soup will do, just as it is.

Spinach, broad bean and artichoke salad

I was inspired to make this salad by the way Italians eat raw baby broad beans with salami, prosciutto or pecorino. The essence of the salad is fresh springiness, so only make it if you can find bouncy young spinach. Theoretically, it would be best to use fresh broad beans, too, but in my experience frozen beans are normally more youthful than the superannuated broad beans sold as fresh. Use only a fraction of the dressing and refrigerate the rest for later use.

ingredients for 2

1 tbsp red wine vinegar

a pinch of dry mustard powder

3 tbsp extra-virgin olive oil

2 tbsp groundnut (or vegetable) oil

1 tbsp walnut oil

FOR THE SALAD

about 150g broad beans (shelled weight)

4 bottled artichoke hearts in oil
drained, patted dry and halved

2 large handfuls of young spinach leaves
washed, trimmed and patted dry

4–6 chestnut mushrooms
wiped clean and thinly sliced

a handful of parsley
leaves roughly chopped

some fine shavings of Parmesan

To make the dressing, whisk together the vinegar, mustard powder and some seasoning, then whisk in the oils to make a thickish emulsion.

For the salad, bring a large saucepan of salted water to a boil and throw in the broad beans. Bring the water back to the boil and cook the beans for 1–2 minutes, or until just tender. Drain and refresh in ice-cold water, then gently squeeze off (and discard) the little mealy jacket from each bean. Pat the kernels dry with kitchen paper. (If you have the time or inclination, griddle the artichoke hearts for a minute or so on each side, over a medium-high heat, to colour them.)

Toss all the ingredients except the Parmesan in a large bowl. Season, using lots of black pepper, then add a little dressing and toss again. The leaves should be glossy but not sodden. Divide the salad between 2 serving plates and scatter the Parmesan shavings on top. Eat immediately.

more you could augment the salad with crumbled dry-fried pancetta or Parma ham. A hunk of hot garlic bread wouldn't go amiss either.

less go gently with the cheese.

Nice easy (raw) things to do with fresh fruit

Unfortunately, almost every desirable pudding you can think of is riddled with sugar, butter, cream or chocolate. With the exception of jelly (see page 167) and sorbet, both of which still include sugar, it's hard to think of a single pudding that can be recommended to someone wanting to lose weight. Fruit, on the other hand, contains fibre, minerals and vitamins, so despite fructose being every bit as calorific as sucrose, it does add something positive to one's diet. I have often read that fruit should be consumed in the morning (rather than later in the day) and not after a heavy meal. I have no idea whether there is any scientific reason for this diktat but I ignore it completely and so far have lived to tell the tale. Personally, I am quite happy to eat most fruits just as they come, but sometimes it's nice to mess around with them.

Bananas can be: sliced, dusted with ground ginger and sprinkled with a little orange juice; sliced and mixed with 1 or 2 chopped dates and some low-fat yoghurt; sliced, lightly dusted with drinking chocolate powder and folded into low-fat vanilla yoghurt.

Figs can be: quartered, opened like a flower and scented with a drop of rosewater or orange flower water; served with thin slices of air-cured ham or tiny chunks of dripping fresh buffalo mozzarella.

Oranges can be: peeled (pith and all) and sliced into rounds, then flavoured with a few cardamom seeds and some chopped raw pistachios; segmented and mixed with chunks of pineapple and 1 or 2 chopped fresh dates; segmented and tossed with grapefruit segments, thin slices of stem ginger and a trickle of ginger syrup.

Strawberries can be: sprinkled very sparingly with balsamic vinegar; dusted lightly with black pepper; sprinkled with rosewater or a few drops of Cointreau; combined with chunks of Charentais or cantaloupe melon and a dash of orange juice; whizzed into a thick purée and served with raspberries, melon, sliced banana or peaches.

Raspberries can be: dropped one by one into a small glass of chilled champagne, and scooped out one by one (using a spoon or clean fingers); mixed with sweet red grapes and a drop of almond extract; combined with white currants, small cubes of watermelon and a dash of rosewater; mixed with blueberries and folded into a spoonful or two of goat's milk yoghurt.

Peaches can be: peeled, sliced and dribbled with fresh raspberry sauce (raspberries whizzed with a little icing sugar and lemon juice); sliced and drowned in a small glass of chilled Prosecco; tumbled with cubes of melon and chopped mint.

Mango and papaya can be: thinly sliced and sprinkled with fresh lime juice; cut into large chunks and tossed with finely sliced stem ginger; cut into slices, mixed with pineapple chunks and dribbled with passion fruit pulp.

Blackberries can be: tossed with cubes of watermelon and a few fresh cob nuts; tumbled with wafer-thin slices of apple and a teaspoon of chopped toasted almonds.

when the GOING gets TOUGH

It is not uncommon for energy levels to dip in the late afternoon and early evening, but for me the urge to eat becomes more feverish than the Yellow River. Five o' clock, and I'm peering in the fridge, opening up kitchen cupboards and checking to see if there's anything edible stashed in my desk drawer. Picture a leopard prowling round its cage waiting for the keeper to throw in a dripping hunk of beef, and that's me – except that I'm not as svelte, or as spotty. The good thing is that over the last 18 months I have not only built up a comprehensive dietary-snack shopping list, I have also developed a few diversionary tactics.

One piece of advice you've probably heard before (and dismissed as either being too facile or completely wacky) is to drink lots of water. I can already feel your eye skipping down the page but stay a moment – please. First, it really is good for your system. We live stressful lives; we eat too much processed food; we don't exercise enough; we jam ourselves into shops, offices and trains, hugger-mugger with every bug out for the killing; and we drink too much alcohol, tea and coffee. All of this puts a great strain on our livers and kidneys, a strain that drinking plenty of water helps to alleviate. (However, don't overdo it; I'm talking about drinking 2-3 litres of water over the course of an entire day, not 8 litres in an hour.) An added bonus is that hydrating your body properly will plump up your skin and bring a sparkle to your eyes. As a guide, and at the risk of straying on to very dodgy, antithetical ground – for a cookery book – the urine excreted from a healthy body should look the colour of modestly priced toilet water, not expensive scent. Secondly, when you are overcome by the urge to eat, stop and ask yourself if you really do feel hungry. It sounds odd, but frequently it's actually thirst you are experiencing, not hunger. There have been many occasions when, once I've stopped to question myself, I've realised that it's liquid I need, not food.

Apart from the late-afternoon slump there are other moments – no, I lie, there are hours, and sometimes even days – when I am overtaken by an appalling desire to devour everything in sight. Fortunately, I have found a number of answers, one of the least attractive being sugar-free chewing gum. Gum is my Nicorette, and I rely on it to masticate my way out of trouble: it helps stifle the desperate need to keep my jaws in motion. Of course, you probably think that people who chew gum are all louts, but Alex Ferguson is not the only person to practise this antisocial habit. Anyway, I am only advocating that you do it in the comfort and privacy of your own home, not out on the streets.

While I am talking down and dirty, I may as well mention low-calorie fizzy drinks. For many years I used to drink Diet Coke (straight from the can – I have some sense of style) at every available opportunity. One day I grew up and saw it for the horribly artificial drink it is. But I can't pretend there aren't times when the idea of yet another glass of water is anathema, especially when my husband is on to his third glass of Pinot Grigio. So, just occasionally, I'll pour myself a cola, forget about the dubious ingredients and enjoy it for nothing other than the frothy spurious pop it is. (And, just for the record, while 'real' Coca-Cola is infinitely better tasting than 'real' Pepsi, the reverse is true of the diet versions, where Pepsi scores hands down – in my opinion.) Your preference may be for something more sophisticated, such as low-calorie bitter lemon, but I do think it is a good idea to have something cold, fizzy and frivolous in the fridge.

Liquid solace aside, it is imperative that you stockpile a large hoard of munchable treats, all of which can be eaten with relative impunity. Never kid yourself that you are somehow immune to snack-attacks. If you're human, they will happen and you must plan for them well in advance. The very worst thing you can do is hope that you can control your hunger pangs (whether genuine or not) with willpower. It simply won't happen and eventually you will lunge for the nearest comestible. And, when you do cave in, it's vital that it's not a bowl of clotted-cream rice pudding you fall upon – simply because that's the only food around. It doesn't matter when you fall foul of the food furies, the fridge must be full of good nibbles that don't disappear in a second and can be stretched out to fill any perilous periods. You will want to assemble your own list of stand-by snacks but overleaf are some of the things that have kept me going through the Twiglet zone. (Is that Freudian or what? I meant to write twilight zone.)

Snack food or not, do exercise the same discretion when selecting suitable emergency food as you would when choosing a nice ripe wedge of Brie. Personally, I am not prepared to lower my standards because I am dieting and I make no apology for constantly banging on about buying the best, whether it's fresh or processed food. To my mind, eating well matters even more when you're dieting than when you're not.

cherry tomatoes Buy Gardener's Delight, tiny Santa plum tomatoes, Vittoria (a bit bigger, these) or marble-sized Jester tomatoes. They all have the necessary sweetness and healthy scrunch of juiciness.

grapes It takes quite a while to strip a big bunch of grapes from its skeleton but, frustratingly (and all too often), it's simply not worth the effort. I've never been a big fan of seedless grapes, but even worse are some of the huge handsome ones (normally green) that come from countries not normally associated with vine-growing. Recently I bought a bunch of these fine-looking fellows and they were quite extraordinary – tough and tasteless. However, Italian muscat grapes, with their luscious, scented flesh, will never disappoint.

cherries You can apply almost everything I've said about grapes to cherries (and plums, nectarines, peaches, apricots and strawberries, for that matter). The finest cherries are grown in England, North America, France or Italy – although, deep into November, I ate some passably decent Argentinian ones. I avoid the Turkish cherries: they invariably have a flaccid texture, dreary flavour, and are frequently blemished. Needless to say, supermarkets seem to stock them in the greatest proliferation. I am also passionate about so-called white cherries (actually madder-splashed yellow), which share the same subtle aromatic sweetness as white peaches.

ready-prepared fresh fruit Whatever the label may say about luxury, finest or exotic, I rarely buy tubs of mixed fresh fruit salad. Almost unfailingly, they comprise crudely cut orange segments, hard wedges of imported apple, a few characterless grapes and the odd chunk of under-ripe melon or a strawberry thrown in for good measure, or notional colour. On the other hand, I like to have some cartons of mango or pineapple chunks tucked in the fridge – do check the mango is fully ripe, though.

smoothies For people who can't stomach a proper breakfast, fruit smoothies make a drinkable alternative. But be careful: good-quality smoothies are made exclusively from the fruit advertised on the main label. I notice that even the best brands are now starting to dilute the featured fruit with cheaper apple juice. Even more importantly, do not be tempted into thinking that yoghurt smoothies are just as 'innocent' as fruit-only smoothies. While a 250ml bottle of the latter contains about 100kcal, the yoghurt-based smoothies contain nearer 250kcal – almost a quarter of your day's ration.

dried fruit I love prunes in sticky tarts, puddings, ice cream or compotes, but find them a bit rich to eat *au nature*. No such caveat applies to dried figs and apricots, although there is a problem with the ones flagged up as 'soft' or 'soaked' or 'snackable'. These squishy masqueraders may be okay for cooking purposes but they are utterly hopeless for those of us seeking an extended, semi-resilient chew: after one sploshy chomp they're gone. My advice is to seek out organic apricots or figs that – so far – don't seem to have fallen prey to unnecessary modification.

seeds Pumpkin, sunflower and sesame seeds are loaded with protein, fibre, magnesium, zinc, iron and vitamins E and B. But they are also very calorific,

owing to the high level of unsaturated (but cholesterol-lowering) fat they contain. The trick is to eat them just a pinch or two at a time, scattered in a salad or soup, or over rice, noodles or cottage cheese. You can also gussy them up by dry-frying a mixture (one packet each of sunflower and pumpkin, plus a small handful of sesame seeds) in a very large frying pan until they stop leaping about and are toasty brown. Then splash them with a little tamari (or light soy sauce) and shake the pan until the seeds are well lacquered. When they have cooled, tip them into an airtight container where they'll keep for weeks, if they don't get eaten first.

liquorice I am not referring to the sweet, squidgy, all-sort type of liquorice but the hard stuff, preferably salty, that the Dutch and Scandinavians adore. It's as tough as bicycle tyres but deeply savoury, and the lingering flavour is very satisfying to the senses. That's if you like liquorice, of course – I can quite see that it falls into that love-hate Marmite category. I also like liquorice twigs (aka Spanish wood), the arboreal version that one chews and sucks to liberate the aromatic liquid.

savoury rice cakes Talking about Marmite, I find the rice cakes that are impregnated with yeast extract extremely useful (I use the word advisedly, they are not exactly gorgeous) when I crave something really savoury. Where the non-dieting me would reach for a crusty white loaf, hack off a couple of doorstep slices and spread them with unsalted butter and a fine smearing of Marmite, the dieting me tucks into a vegetable extract rice cake (or two). Not too convincing a substitute but better than nothing.

Philadelphia Light Snacks Truly, this combo of high-baked grissini (bread sticks) and cream cheese (albeit only a tiny reservoir) is one of the most genuinely toothsome unadulterated diet snacks on the market. Adding up to only about 100kcal a pack, they fill those must-have-bread-and-cheese moments very well.

chocolate cereal bars This is a big-red-warning, siren-howling zone. The truth is that many, indeed most, cereal bars are hideously high in carbohydrates, despite what the labels may say about their energy- or health-enhancing properties. I will go so far as to say that many of them are a real sham, pretending they are superior to ordinary confectionery when they are equally high in sugar and fat. The cereal bar I favour is called Geo, and I like it partly because the ingredients are organic and partly because it contains only 120kcal – but mostly because it tastes bloody good.

rice and corn cakes I am rather embarrassed about sharing this secret with you, but I don't know if could have sustained my diet if Snack-a-Jacks hadn't been invented. Relatively free of crap, I actually like they way they taste and, more importantly, the way they scrunch. At 50kcal per jumbo cake, I find them invaluable, particularly the caramel and chocolate varieties. I am not so keen on the little Snack-a-Jacks (somehow the flavour/texture ratio is not as satisfactory) nor the cheese or barbecue-flavoured jumbo cakes. As for the apple and cinnamon flavour, the least said the better.

milk lollies Oddly enough, not all ice cream bars or lollies are loaded sky-high with calories. The biggest difficulty is that because so many of them are made for an international market it's rare to find a breakdown of the contents, as is compulsory on European packaging. (Except, weirdly enough, anything weighing less than 40g.) I regret the passing of the original Bounty Bar ice cream because it was quite 'cheap', calorifically. Better still, it came in two chunks (just like the confectionery), which meant you could eat one and save one. Sadly, it's now sold as one big slab, so I rely mostly on children's milk lollies for a quick fix. Although the ingredients are quite virtuous I don't kid myself that's the real reason for the modest 90kcal calorie count – it's simply because they are so tiny.

sherbert fountains Shockingly low in calories, a whole tube, complete with liquorice 'straw', only accounts for 88kcal. This could be because it's impossible to suck anything up through the permanently clogged 'straw' or it could be that the tubes are not even half-full of sherbert. I seem to remember them being much more generously packed when I was little, but then so were Pizza Express pizzas much larger – yes, I know they've put them up by 20%, without admitting they had diminished in size over the years, but I remain unconvinced. Anyway, I love sherbert fountains, not just for the nebulous, explosive mouth-feel or the taste of liquorice, but because the 'Roman candle' packaging is utterly brilliant.

crystallised ginger You have to go really gently on this one because the lumps of ginger are literally caked in sugar. Try to brush off as much as possible and don't eat more than a couple of chunks a day. It's terrific stuff, though, and very good for the digestion. I'm trying to justify myself; I don't really care about its health-giving attributes, just the fierce, nostril-tingling flavour.

Green & Black's chocolate Here, I am talking specifically about the 20g bars of organic milk chocolate and Maya Gold dark chocolate. While a

'normal' size bar carries a stonking half-day's worth of calories, each of these titchy bars contains around 100kcal. As a twice a week treat they are really helpful – and because the chocolate is such good quality, a little goes a long way.

gherkins Being merely cucumbers with attitude, gherkins are fabulously low in calories and, therefore, great for scoffing. They are also as crunchy as hell and, depending on the pickle, have a touch of sweetness about them. You have to be a bit picky when choosing your brand though, as some are far too vinegary, some too small (cornichons don't do it for me in this context) and some too flabby. The latter defect may be because the gherkins are big and 'seedy' or because they've been hanging around too long: even unopened, gherkins do not go on for ever. Find your favourite wally and you'll have a friend for life.

flying saucers Am I the only adult who has regressed in middle-age to buying children's sweets? When I was a kid, I adored flying saucers and the way the rice-paper dissolved and clung to my palate, while the sherbert fizzed and filled my mouth. Now I'm old, I still love the pale neon colours, the tough shiny casing that melts into soft pap, and the feel of the sherbert as it explodes. I especially like the fact that a whole bag only weighs 30g, which is partly why they account for so few calories. A decent-sized pork pie weighs about half a pound and, even if it weren't chock-full of saturated fat, would tot up to a hefty number of calories. This is something to bear in mind, whatever it is you are eating.

Apart from keeping a stock of saintly snacks, I also practise the dark art of repackaging high-calorie treats into small portions. Take, for example, Green & Black's organic mint chocolate which, sadly, doesn't come in 20g bars. When I simply have to have some, I break it into 2-square bits, wrap each chunk in clingfilm and store them in the fridge door. Knowing there is a stash of chocolate in the house counteracts the feeling of deprivation that so often accompanies a diet: parcelling the chocolate into moderate 100kcal portions acts as a barrier against wolfing down the whole bar in one go. The result is that I am less likely to come careering out of the dietary straitjacket and binge.

Still on the subject of sweet temptation, it is absolutely vital to keep adequate stocks of emergency snacks in the car. Those petrol stations with their wall-to-wall displays of chocolate, and fridges full of (horrible) all-day breakfast sandwiches, are as mesmeric to the average slimmer as a sleeping antelope to a lion. It was while searching for an atlas in my husband's car that I came across the solution to why he remained so podgy around the waist when I knew I was feeding him blameless grub: I counted 11 – yes 11 – sweetie wrappers in the driver's side pocket. It's not just your mobile phone you should remember to switch off when you enter the forecourt but the food-seeking part of your brain.

A final word of warning. Having entreated you to stockpile plenty of snacks, I must also mention the obvious disadvantage of having a house stuffed with them, however non-fattening – YOU MUST NOT EAT THEM ALL AT ONCE! I apologise for the capital letters and the exclamation mark, but it really is no good having a pack of caramel-flavoured rice cakes in the cupboard, each biscuit decent and restrained in its 50kcal content, and then scoffing twelve of them in one go.

So much about dieting is to do with kidding one's psyche into believing it's feast-time, not famine. This is why I recommend starting a diet with a trip to a health farm, if you can afford the time and money. Being denied any carbohydrate at all means that you will appreciate even the smallest morsel of bread or rice when you emerge. No longer will you consider having a second helping of buttery mashed potato along with a fried egg and some greasy pork sausages, instead you will be delighted if you can have the smallest baked potato with a mere smattering of cottage cheese and herbs. So, go lightly on those snacks and mix up the carbohydrate-high(ish) ones with the really low-calories ones – in other words, if you have a Philly snack at 4.30, don't follow it half an hour later with a Geo bar, but have a packet of cherry tomatoes instead.

BIG food, SLOW food

A famous gastronome, A J Liebling, once said, "I like flavours that know their own minds." I am with him all the way. Flavour is incredibly important in my daily diet, but that's not the only reason I am so drawn to Asian-style cooking. I say Asian-style, rather than Asian, because although you'll find oyster or black bean sauce adding their inimitable funky flavours to many of these recipes, the amount of oil that goes into a genuine Chinese stir-fry is alarming. As for traditional Indian food, with its plethora of gorgeous breads and ghee-saturated sauces, it's pretty much the antithesis of what you should eat if you're trying to lose weight. So, with a few exceptions, it's Japan and Thailand that I plunder for the type of spirited, invigorating food that whips the taste buds into submission. As well as employing brilliant flavours, their cooking is also superlatively healthy, being predicated largely on fresh fish, poultry, meat and vegetables. In fact, the Japanese hardly ever eat desserts, except for ice cream, a Western habit picked up during the American occupation after World War II. It doesn't bother me: Japanese chefs prepare such stunningly perfect plates of fantastically cut fresh fruit, I hardly notice the absence of treacle tart.

But it's not flavour alone that explains why this chapter includes so many Asian-style recipes: it's also because you can eat most of the food in such large quantity. A central tenet of my dieting success is that volume is vital. For me, it's a no-hoper if I have to leave the table feeling as if I haven't had my money's worth. I soon discovered that the quickest way to do just that was to blow nigh-on 400kcal on three ounces of Cheddar. Have you any idea how little that is? Well, I'll tell you because I've just gone into the kitchen to check. A three-ounce chunk of Cheddar measures three inches long and one inch wide, and that's just a tad bigger than a pack of chewing gum. At a conservative estimate, I reckon it would take no more than four mouthfuls to consume the lot – say, two minutes? It leaves a heck of a long evening looming. I can't be doing with that: my main meal has to be really substantial, and time-consuming to eat.

Despite my 'big food' recipes being very satisfying, I still think it's a good idea to have at least two courses, if not three, for the main meal of the day. This could mean finishing with a plate of fruit or a small pot of a sweet, low-calorie dessert. I am very partial to some of the Marks & Spencer range of Count On Us puddings. I know it's very risky mentioning specific examples, given the notorious disappearing act that so many supermarket lines perform, but

Count On Us mousse has been around for a few years, so I think it's probably here to stay. The chocolate mousse is particularly good, whether plain or flavoured with mint, but I also like the (admittedly chemically enhanced) tiramisu, and the surprisingly sophisticated mocha dessert that comes in a good-looking glass.

If you don't share my sweet tooth, have a starter instead. (Although I am doubtful that anyone who doesn't like sugary things needs to be on a diet at all; I haven't met many fat people who don't care a fig about puddings.)

I happen to be particularly partial to starters: I love the whole notion of nibbling at something small and inviting as a precursor to something more substantial. It could be anything from a few slices of smoked salmon, raw marinated scallops, gravlax or half a smoked trout; a prawn or crab cocktail (with just a scant tablespoon of low-fat mayo let down to dressing consistency with a slurp of skimmed milk); a cucumber and dill salad with low-fat yoghurt and dill or mustard dressing, again let down with skimmed milk; a medium-sized bowl of soup (assuming your main course is 'dry'); a few slices of Parma ham with or without melon, fresh figs, papaya or pear; beef fillet carpaccio with a handful of rocket; tomato and basil salad with half a torn mozzarella ball, lots of seasoning and a dash of olive oil; a plate of asparagus (hot or cold) with just a few spots of balsamic vinegar; or low-fat hummus with raw vegetables.

Whatever you choose, you will find that the psychological benefit of having a 'proper' meal is enormous. I keep repeating it, but unless your diet is compatible with a normal adult lifestyle, you will soon start bunking off and scoffing everything in sight. Even if you're not actually spoiling yourself, you must not feel that you are actively depriving yourself. There's a big difference.

BIG FOOD RECIPES

You only have to look at these recipes to get the gist of what I mean: big bowls of mussels, their Quink ink-coloured shells stacked to the heavens; huge broth-pots crammed with chicken, prawns and tofu, as well as rice or noodles and enough vegetables to fill Covent Garden; mountainous salads, jangling with different textures and flavours; and voluminous soups, stuffed full of wonderful flavour but so meagre in calories you can happily go back for more. All of it big food in quantity, big food in flavour and big food in its satisfaction quota. And, no, there isn't any bread to dunk, crunch or mop up the juices, but you won't miss it. The (mostly) Asian-style recipes include enough starch to provide the necessary bit of ballast (as do the more traditional European soups).

The only caveat is that you will also need some big pots. Most domestic kitchens are very scantily equipped when it comes to large-sized saucepans, not to mention colanders, measuring jugs, spoons, frying pans and sieves. For some reason manufacturers and retailers seem to think that only professional kitchens need large-scale equipment, but this is complete nonsense. You don't need an abnormally sized family to want to cook a big pot of soup, or a large quantity of spinach (bearing in mind that it flops down to nothing), or a decent-sized braised chicken, or a lavish quantity of pasta – to name just a few everyday dishes. If you have any hope of cooking well, then you must have at least one huge (say 6 litre) saucepan, with lid, and one (36–38 cm) wok, frying pan or sauté pan, and a colander. Add a pair of long-handled chef's tongs, some big wooden spoons and plastic spatulas, a capacious roasting tin, and a couple of really heavy baking sheets of similar size, and you're laughing – or cooking (or both).

Most of the following recipes have emerged from my diet diary, a thick black page-to-a-day affair in which I record what I eat, together with quickly sketched recipes. I am aware that many of them are variations on a theme, depending on what's available. I make no apology, because this, surely, is real life: opening up the fridge door, gazing at the contents (or lack of them) in bewildered wonderment and slowly building up an idea of what to do with what's there. Actually, I rather like this kind of 'necessity' cooking, as long as it's not too late in the evening and I'm not completely knackered. It helps that I always keep the store cupboard stocked with loads of bottled sauces (by which I do not mean Chicken Tonight, but soy, oyster, mushroom sauces, and the like) as well as different noodles, rice and pulses. But the point I am making is that you shouldn't dismiss a particular recipe just because you haven't got any, say, sugar snaps. A recipe should be viewed as a cooking guide, not as a prescription for mind-altering drugs.

Squash, bean and onion soup (with a bit of cabbage)

I cannot see any point in making a tiddly amount of soup. It's one of the few things that gets better as it gets older (which is not the same as geriatric), and I love the warm feeling of security that goes with knowing there's a big pot of home-made soup tucked up in the fridge. As usual, nature has got it right, rewarding us with all those glorious brassicas, squashes and root vegetables (swede being the only aberration) just when we are desperate for some hearty, sweet-edged veg to turn into comforting slop.

ingredients for 4

1 tbsp olive oil

15g unsalted butter

2 very large Spanish onions
roughly chopped

3–4 garlic cloves
crushed and roughly chopped

2 tsp juniper berries
crushed

a few gratings of whole nutmeg

1 butternut squash (or other squash)
peeled and cut into large bite-sized chunks

2 tbsp Marigold Swiss vegetable bouillon powder

1 (420g) can of cannellini (or borlotti) beans
drained and rinsed

1 pointed cabbage
trimmed, quartered, cored and sliced crossways into thin ribbons

(optional) a handful of flat leaf parsley
roughly chopped

Heat the oil and butter in a very large saucepan over a low-medium flame. Throw in the onions and garlic, and cook for 10 minutes, stirring frequently. Stir in the juniper and nutmeg, and cook for 1 minute. Add the squash and cook for 5 minutes.

Put in the stock powder, 2.5 litres of water and some seasoning. Turn up the heat, bring the soup to a boil, half-covered, then simmer the soup for 15 minutes. Add the beans and cabbage and cook for a further 10–15 minutes, or until the vegetables are tender. Stir in the (optional) parsley, check the seasoning and serve.

A spring alternative
Omit the cabbage, juniper and nutmeg, but add 150g chopped rhubarb and 3 pinches each of ground coriander, cinnamon and ginger and 2 of chilli powder. Whizz to a smooth purée, then chuck in 2 cans of Whole Earth organic baked beans. Reheat and serve.

Homely minestrone soup

I make no apology for this recipe having appeared in print before – it's simply one of the best, easiest and most satisfying soups, and I can't get enough of it. It also improves with maturity. Rather than issuing endless instructions, take it as read that all the vegetables must be rinsed thoroughly, with tough outer layers, inedible peel and roots or cores removed where necessary.

ingredients for 10+

3 tbsp olive oil

2 large Spanish onions
cut into medium dice

4 garlic cloves
crushed and finely chopped

3 leeks
halved lengthways and finely sliced

1 fennel bulb
cut into medium dice

4 celery sticks
cut into medium dice

4 medium carrots
cut into small dice

4 tbsp Marigold Swiss vegetable bouillon powder

500ml tomato passata

2 sprigs of fresh thyme (or oregano)

4 medium courgettes
cut into medium dice

¼ Savoy cabbage
cored and sliced into thin ribbons

100g small pasta (e.g. stars, shells)

2 (420g) cans of cannellini beans
rinsed and drained

a handful each of parsley and basil
roughly chopped

Heat the oil in a huge saucepan over a low-medium flame. Stir in the onion, garlic and leeks, and cook for 5 minutes. Stir in the fennel, celery and carrots, and cook gently for 8–10 minutes, until softened. Add the stock powder, 4 litres of water, the passata, thyme and seasoning, and bring to a boil. Reduce the heat and simmer gently for 30 minutes, half-covered. Add the courgettes, cabbage and pasta, and bring back to a boil, uncovered. Add more water if the soup is too thick. Simmer for 15 minutes, then add the beans and cook for 10–15 minutes. Stir in the herbs and season. The soup is ready when a happy alliance has formed. It can be served immediately but I like minestrone best when it has rested for a day.

Tofu, rice and pak choi broth

Nothing stupendous – just a very satisfying Eastern-inspired muddle of great flavours in a light broth. Do all the cutting and chopping first as the recipe only takes a few minutes of actual cooking time.

ingredients for 2

1 big 'thumb' of root ginger
peeled and grated

3 garlic cloves
crushed and finely chopped

2 mild red chillies
de-seeded and finely sliced

8 spring onions
trimmed, and each one cut at
an angle into three

**2 sachets of dashi stock powder
(or 3 tsp Marigold Swiss vegetable
bouillon powder)**
dissolved in about 1 litre boiling water

30g basmati rice

4 medium pak choi
trimmed and quartered lengthways

100g fresh shiitake
halved or quartered, depending on size

1 small carrot
shaved into fine strips with
a potato peeler

2 tbsp dark soy sauce

1 (250g) carton of firm silken tofu
drained and cut into large chunks

1 sheet of nori
toasted and cut into thin strips

Put the ginger, garlic, chillies and spring onions into a very large wok, preferably non-stick. Add the stock and rice, then set the wok over a medium-high flame and bring the contents to a boil. Reduce the heat and simmer strongly for 3 minutes, stirring occasionally.

Stir in the pak choi and shiitake and cook them for about 5 minutes. Add the carrot strips and soy sauce, and stir thoroughly. Put in the tofu, without stirring this time, then cover the wok (with a lid or foil) and simmer for 1–2 minutes.

When the tofu is hot, carefully scoop it out and put it in the bottom of 2 large bowls, then pile everything else on top. Scatter with the nori and serve immediately.

Mushroom broth + prawn and pork wontons

Although I've geared most of the recipes in this chapter for only two people, I don't think it's worth making the wontons for so few, so this one will feed four. You can buy the wonton wrappers from the freezer cabinet in Chinese or Asian stores and some good supermarkets stock them too. Failing that, you could make little meatballs of the prawn and pork mixture and poach them in the broth, naked as the day they were born. Either way, it all adds up to a really gutsy bowlful of food.

ingredients for 4

250g peeled raw tiger prawns

115g finely minced lean pork

3 (canned) water chestnuts
rinsed, patted dry and roughly chopped

2 garlic cloves
crushed

1 'thumb' of root ginger
peeled and grated

a small handful of fresh coriander
leaves only

1 tbsp Japanese soy sauce

2 tsp sake (or dry sherry)

1 packet of wonton wrappers
defrosted, if frozen

FOR THE BROTH

2 litres of shiitake broth
made up as instructed on the bottle

½ Chinese cabbage
halved, cored and sliced crossways
into thin ribbons

2 tbsp Japanese soy sauce

**2 tbsp Chinese rice wine (or sake
or dry sherry)**

a large handful of fresh coriander
leaves roughly chopped

4 spring onions
topped, tailed and cut at an angle
into large pieces

Whizz all the wonton ingredients, except the wrappers, into a coarse paste. Put a teaspoon of the mixture into the middle of a wrapper, brush the edges with water, then seal the wonton by bringing 2 opposite corners together, then the other 2, and pressing the edges firmly together. Repeat until all the mixture has been used up, then refrigerate the wontons on a tray until required. (They can be made up to 24 hours ahead.)

Pour the shiitake broth into a very large saucepan and bring it to a boil over a medium-high flame.

Add the Chinese cabbage, soy sauce, rice wine, coriander and half the spring onions, and simmer strongly for 3 minutes, uncovered, stirring occasionally. Add the wontons and simmer for a further 3–5 minutes, or until they float to the top and the wrappers look cooked. (It's worth testing one – if the filling feels smooth and pappy, rather than nubbly, they need more time.)

Carefully spoon the wontons into 4 warmed bowls, then add the broth, vegetables and the remaining spring onions.

Prawn laksa

This is yet another recipe that looks more daunting than it actually is, although you could take a short cut by buying ready-made laksa paste: it's not bad, but lacks the real sting and zing of the home-made stuff. Whichever type you use, there will still be a world of difference between this laksa, which seethes with vivid and intriguing flavours, and the tubs of rich, sickly ready-made laksa you find in supermarkets.

ingredients for 4

FOR THE PASTE

1 lemon grass stalk
inner leaves roughly chopped,
outer leaves reserved for the broth

2–3 Thai chillies, to taste
halved and de-seeded

3 garlic cloves
crushed and roughly chopped

1 'thumb' of root ginger
peeled and roughly sliced

1 large shallot
roughly chopped

a large handful of fresh coriander
leaves and stalks roughly chopped

1 tsp ground coriander

2 pinches of ground turmeric

FOR THE SOUPY BIT

250g medium egg noodles

750g raw shell-on tiger prawns
peeled and all the debris reserved

4 tsp Marigold Swiss vegetable bouillon powder

1.2 litres hot water

1 tbsp toasted sesame oil

1 (400ml) can of coconut milk

2 tbsp Thai fish sauce (nam pla)

about 200g fresh beansprouts

3 bushy sprigs of fresh mint
leaves bundled up and sliced

a handful of fresh coriander
leaves roughly chopped

(to serve) 4 lime wedges

Put all the paste ingredients in a blender (or mini-food processor) with 4 tablespoons of water and whizz into a thick, slightly coarse sludge, scraping down the sides of the bowl occasionally. Refrigerate for up to 72 hours.

Cook the noodles according to the instructions on the packet, drain, and rinse under cold water. Leave them to one side.

To make the broth, put all the prawn debris (including heads) into a large saucepan with the reserved outer lemon grass leaves. Add the stock powder and hot water, and bring to a boil. Reduce the heat and simmer, uncovered, for 15–20 minutes. Strain the resulting stock through a damp muslin-lined sieve, discarding the debris.

Put a very large saucepan over a low-medium flame and, when it is hot, add the sesame oil. Scrape every last bit of the laksa paste into the saucepan and cook it for 1–2 minutes, stirring almost constantly. Increase the heat to medium and then stir in the prawn stock, coconut milk and Thai fish sauce.

Cover the pan and bring the contents to a boil, then reduce the heat and simmer the broth for 15–20 minutes. Add the prawns and cook them for 1 minute, uncovered, then throw in the

reserved noodles and the beansprouts and continue simmering for 1–2 minutes, or until everything is piping hot.

Divide the laksa among the serving bowls, making sure everybody has their fair share of prawns. Strew the chopped mint and coriander over each bowl and perch a wedge of lime on top (to be squeezed into the broth).

Chilli squid and ribbon veg salad

I think we have Chinese restaurants, not to mention Greek holidays, to thank for squid being an accepted part of our gastronomic lexicon: most supermarkets stock cleaned squid sacs (or hoods). Apart from the marination time, everything happens in minutes, so make sure the ingredients are all prepared and ready to go. Spritzed with lime juice, chilli and coriander, this salad is as zingy as it gets.

ingredients for 2

275g small squid sacs
cut in half lengthways to make shield-shaped pieces

1 tbsp fresh lime juice

1 tsp Thai fish sauce (nam pla)

4 tbsp sweet chilli sauce

a drop of groundnut (or vegetable) oil

FOR THE DRESSING AND SALAD

1 tbsp fresh lime juice

a large pinch of caster sugar

1 tbsp groundnut (or vegetable) oil

1 large carrot
topped and tailed

1 large (very fresh) courgette
topped and tailed

1 small red pepper
de-seeded and cut into paper-thin slices

a small handful of fresh coriander
leaves chopped

Score a shallow criss-cross pattern on the inside surface of the squid, then put into a non-reactive dish. Combine the lime juice, fish sauce and chilli sauce, pour it over the squid and toss well. Massage the marinade in and refrigerate for 3 to 12 hours.

To make the dressing, whisk the lime juice, sugar and oil together with some seasoning to taste. Using a potato peeler, sweep down the carrot and courgette to make a pile of very fine strips, then toss them in the dressing with the red pepper, and leave for up to 30 minutes. (They will start to 'cook' if you leave them too long – so don't.)

Heat a very lightly oiled heavy frying pan (or griddle) over a high flame. Drain the squid, discarding the marinade, and when the pan is smoking-hot, cook the squid (in batches, if necessary) for 1–2 minutes, turning the pieces halfway through. Combine the squid and coriander with the vegetables, toss and serve.

more add 100g cold cooked udon or egg noodles for extra bulk.

Thai-style mussels

As we all know, part of the pleasure of tucking into a bowl of mussels is not just disposing of the sweet flesh but the great puddle of liquor left at the end. With my self-imposed veto on bread, mopping up the juices is out of the question so I've had to find a way round it. It's quite simple, I've changed continents. Whereas it's de rigueur with moules marinière to dunk crusty hunks of baguette into the wine-infused juices, the thought of bread with an Asian-style dish is anathema – soup spoons will do just fine. Authentically, the broth should contain both galangal and kaffir lime leaves, but these can be hard to come by if you live in the sticks. Here, I've used ginger instead of the galangal (the same amount): if you can find any lime leaves, use 2, very finely sliced. A few torn leaves of Thai (holy) basil would also be good, but don't worry if you can't find that either (grow some – it's easy).

ingredients for 2

300ml fish (or vegetable or chicken) stock

2 garlic cloves
crushed and finely chopped

1 Thai chilli
de-seeded and finely chopped

1 tbsp Thai fish sauce (nam pla)

1 tbsp oyster sauce

1 small 'thumb' of root ginger
peeled and grated

1 stick of lemon grass
inner leaves finely chopped, outer left whole

1.5kg live mussels
well rinsed, beards removed and any open mussels discarded

a small handful of fresh coriander
leaves roughly chopped

Put all the ingredients, except the mussels and coriander, into a huge saucepan. Bring the contents to a boil over a high heat then tip in the mussels. Cover the pan immediately and cook the mussels for 3–4 minutes, shaking the pan vigorously every minute or so, until they have opened. Do not over-cook the mussels or the flesh will be dry and mealy.

Remove (and discard) the outer lemon grass leaves and any closed mussels. Divide the mussels and broth between 2 serving bowls, strew with coriander and eat at once.

N.B. If the mussels are very heavy, it could be because they are quite sandy inside. In that case, cook the mussels separately (in an empty, hot pan), then strain the juices before combining them with the Thai-flavoured stock. Bring the liquid back to the boil, add the coriander and reunite it with the mussels.

One-pan chicken, sugar snaps and tamarind

I nearly always have chicken and prawns in the fridge: together with some key base flavours, like garlic and ginger, it means there's always a meal ready to knock up in minutes. For this recipe, you may also like to try lean pork tenderloin (fillet). If you can't find any tamarind, add a spoonful of honey and a squeeze of lime juice instead – the combination is better than good. As with all quick-cooking, multiple-ingredient recipes, it's vital to have everything prepared and ready to put in the pan when it's needed – or you'll end up with a soggy mess.

ingredients for 2

1 tbsp groundnut (or vegetable) oil

2 skinless chicken breasts
cut at an angle into thin slices

1 small onion
cut into medium dice

3 garlic cloves
crushed and finely chopped

3 celery sticks
trimmed and cut into medium dice

1 red pepper
de-seeded and cut into medium dice

1 'thumb' of root ginger
peeled and grated

1 tbsp toasted sesame oil

150g fresh shiitake
wiped clean and halved or quartered

a large handful of sugar snaps
rinsed

2 tbsp tamarind sauce

1 tbsp soy sauce

1 tbsp Thai fish sauce (nam pla)

Heat a very large non-stick wok (or frying pan) over a medium-high flame. Add the oil and, when it's hot, tip in the chicken. Cook it for 2 minutes, stirring frequently.

Throw in the onion, garlic and celery, and cook for 2 minutes, stirring almost constantly. Add the red pepper and ginger, and cook for another 2–3 minutes, still stirring.

Add the sesame oil, shiitake and sugar snaps, and continue to stir-fry for 2–3 minutes. Finally pour in the tamarind, soy and Thai fish sauces. Stir and cook for 2–3 minutes, or until everything is piping hot and the sugar snaps have lost their rawness but are still on the crunchy side of cooked.

Gingered pork and scallops

One of the most popular dishes on our menu at the Crown and Castle is slow-roast pork belly. We use locally reared Gloucester Old Spot, which has a fantastic flavour and makes great crackling. We then serve the pork with anything from spicy lentils to a shellfish broth jangling with mussels or clams. A few guests register slight consternation at the notion of eating meat with fish, but it's not considered at all odd in many countries, from Spain to China. The proof is in the pudding (or the pork), and most people who try it are happily surprised at how good the combination tastes.

ingredients for 2

115g fine egg noodles

1 tbsp cornflour

3 tbsp dry sherry

1 tbsp soy sauce

1 tbsp groundnut (or vegetable) oil

2 spring onions
trimmed and cut at an angle into fine slices

1 garlic clove
crushed and finely chopped

1 small mild red chilli
de-seeded and finely chopped

1 small red pepper
de-seeded and and chopped into small dice

1 big 'thumb' of root ginger
peeled and grated

about 200g pork fillet (tenderloin)
trimmed and cut across the grain into thin strips

150g fresh queen scallops

Cook the noodles according to the instructions on the packet, drain, rinse and set aside.

Whisk the cornflour together with 125ml cold water, the sherry and soy sauce, then set aside.

Heat a large non-stick wok (or frying pan) over a medium-high flame. Add the oil and, when it is hot, throw in the spring onions, garlic, chilli, red pepper and ginger. Cook for 1–2 minutes, stirring constantly, then add the pork and continue to stir-fry for 3–4 minutes.

Add the scallops and cook them for 1 minute, still keeping everything moving. Pour the cornflour mixture into the pan and, when the sauce boils and thickens, throw in the noodles. Give everything a thorough toss and serve as soon as the noodles are piping hot.

Chicken, shiitake and miso broth

Miso paste is the most astonishing stuff. It looks like a tub of wet sand but tastes of sweet, earthy mystery. Here, my usual wintry suspects – chicken, mushrooms and cabbage – are transformed by a couple of spoonfuls of the wonder stuff.

ingredients for 2

1.5 litres hot water

2 tbsp Marigold Swiss vegetable bouillon powder

8 fresh shiitake
wiped clean, trimmed and quartered

1 'thumb' of root ginger
peeled and grated

1 lemon grass stalk
inner leaves only, finely chopped

2 garlic cloves
crushed and finely chopped

2 tbsp miso paste (light or dark)

¼ Savoy (or Chinese) cabbage
cored and sliced crossways into thin ribbons

2 skinless cooked chicken breasts
torn into little-finger-size shreds

a bundle of rice noodles

a handful of fresh coriander
leaves roughly chopped

(to serve) a dash of Japanese soy sauce

Put the hot water and stock powder into a very large saucepan and bring to a boil over a medium-high flame. Stir in the shiitake, ginger, lemon grass, garlic and miso paste. Reduce the heat and simmer strongly for 3 minutes. Add the cabbage and simmer for a further 3 minutes. Add the chicken, rice noodles and coriander, and simmer for 1 minute.

Remove the pan from the heat and leave the broth to stand for a further 2–3 minutes.

Divide the contents of the pan between 2 deep bowls, season with soy sauce to taste, and serve.

SLOW FOOD RECIPES

For someone on a diet, finishing a meal only minutes after starting it is both depressing and disastrous, given that the subject of food (or the possible lack of it) is uppermost in one's brain. The thought of endless hours to fill before the next bout of eating can commence is not good for the soul. One obvious answer is to stretch out the eating process for as long as possible, but there's another ploy to consider – extend the preparation time, too.

Many of my recipes appear to involve a lot of work. Actually, hardly any of them require great skill, nor do they take much time to cook, but some of the ingredients lists are undeniably lengthy. Obviously this is partly to do with my desire to add as much flavour and texture to a recipe as possible but, funnily enough, it's also because it means I can be actively and fruitfully involved with food, without actually eating it. Yes, of course there are times when I am in a rush or too tired to think about cooking. Then, like anyone else, I want some food to appear in front of me instantly, and if that involves ripping off a lid rather than cutting up a carrot, well so be it. But there's no doubt it's a thousand times more satisfactory to chop, slice and stir one's own carefully garnered batch of ingredients.

Serving food that's messy and fiddly to eat also helps fill up the time. Unlike a hamburger, it takes more than a few desultory bites to put paid to a pint of prawns or a *plateau de fruits de mer*. In fact, eating shellfish, generally, is a brilliant way to spin out a meal in convivial fashion. All that cracking, shelling, peeling and extracting takes for ever. Then, in between each mouthful, you have to stop to wipe your fingers or lick them (more food – good), not to mention identify the next target for attack. If you don't share my passion for shellfish, there are always chicken wings, lamb chops or game birds to pick at, tease and twiddle. Then there's the supporting act. I like to have a plate piled high with asparagus, sprouting broccoli or French beans, and eat them with my fingers, one by one. Or if it's salad, then it must be vast. As long as there's no starch involved and precious little dressing, labouring through a huge bowl of interesting leaves tossed with raw sliced vegetables is both time-consuming and tiring. Just what a dieter needs.

An asparagus feast + soft-boiled eggs

There are many good things about living in Suffolk and being able to pig out, cheaply, on the most beautiful asparagus is one of them. At home we are surrounded by asparagus fields, which look completely empty until you study the light, dusty earth closely and notice there is the odd spear thrusting through the soil. Then you look more closely and see another and another – and suddenly you realise the earth is riven with stealthy herbaceous erections.

Of course, there is nothing as glorious to eat with hot asparagus as unctuous lemony hollandaise – but it's hardly conducive to losing weight. Faced with yet another plate of plain, unadorned asparagus, I decided I had to find an alternative: eggs, with molten runny yolks, were the obvious candidates, although non-dieters may want to anoint their asparagus with a little melted butter, too.

Don't bother with all that nonsense of cooking asparagus in vertical bundles: it cooks perfectly well lying down and loose, in a capacious saucepan. Just make sure all the tips are pointing the same way.

ingredients for 2

1 kg English asparagus
woody ends trimmed off

4 large free-range eggs
at room temperature

You will need to cook the asparagus and eggs simultaneously. For the asparagus, bring a large saucepan of salted water to a boil and put in the spears. Bring the water back to a boil, immediately reduce the heat and simmer the asparagus, uncovered, for 3–5 minutes, or until just tender. (To test, pierce the thickest part of a stalk with the point of a small knife.) Remove the asparagus using tongs and lay it on a double-folded tea towel to mop up every drop of moisture.

While the asparagus is cooking, put the eggs into a small pan filled with enough cold water to cover them. Bring the water to a boil over a high flame then immediately reduce the heat and simmer the eggs, half-covered, for exactly 2 minutes 45 seconds – oh, go on, 3 minutes will be okay, but not a second longer. (This will produce just-set whites and runny yolks.)

To serve, divide the asparagus between 2 warmed plates and season with a little salt and lots of black pepper. Put the eggs into egg cups and dip the spears into the yolks, then scoop the whites out and eat the remaining asparagus with a knife and fork.

Roast quail + 5-spice marinade

You have to be fairly insensitive to eat quail – they are so small and vulnerable-looking. For the stout-hearted, however, gnawing on the tiny bones to extract the delicate morsels of flesh is a tedious delight.

ingredients for 2

4 oven-ready quail

FOR THE MARINADE

3 tbsp sake (or dry sherry)

2 tbsp oyster sauce

1 tbsp Japanese soy sauce

1 tbsp sesame oil

3 pinches of 5-spice powder

2 pinches of caster sugar

2 dashes of sweet chilli sauce

FOR THE STUFFING

4 spring onions
trimmed and cut roughly in four

3 garlic cloves
crushed

1 'thumb' of root ginger
peeled and grated

Put the quail in a close-fitting, non-reactive dish. Whisk the marinade ingredients together and set aside. To make the stuffing, combine the ingredients and chop (or whizz) them coarsely. Dab the stuffing inside the birds, pour over the marinade and leave the quail in a cool place for 4 to 12 hours, turning them occasionally.

Preheat the oven to 220°C fan/gas mark 8. Remove the birds from the marinade (reserving it), then put them on a very large, doubled sheet of cooking foil, dull-side out, and season them. Draw up the foil to make a well-sealed but roomy pouch, and place it on a sturdy baking sheet. Cook the quail for 15 minutes. Meanwhile, pour the marinade into a small saucepan and boil it for a few minutes over a high heat, uncovered, until it is shiny and slightly sticky. Unwrap the pouch and spread open the foil. Brush the quail with the marinade, then continue to roast them, exposed, for about 15 minutes, or until they are glistening and browned. Pour any juices back into the marinade.

Serve the quail with the marinade spooned over, and a bowl of Asian-style salad – see the recipe on page 162.

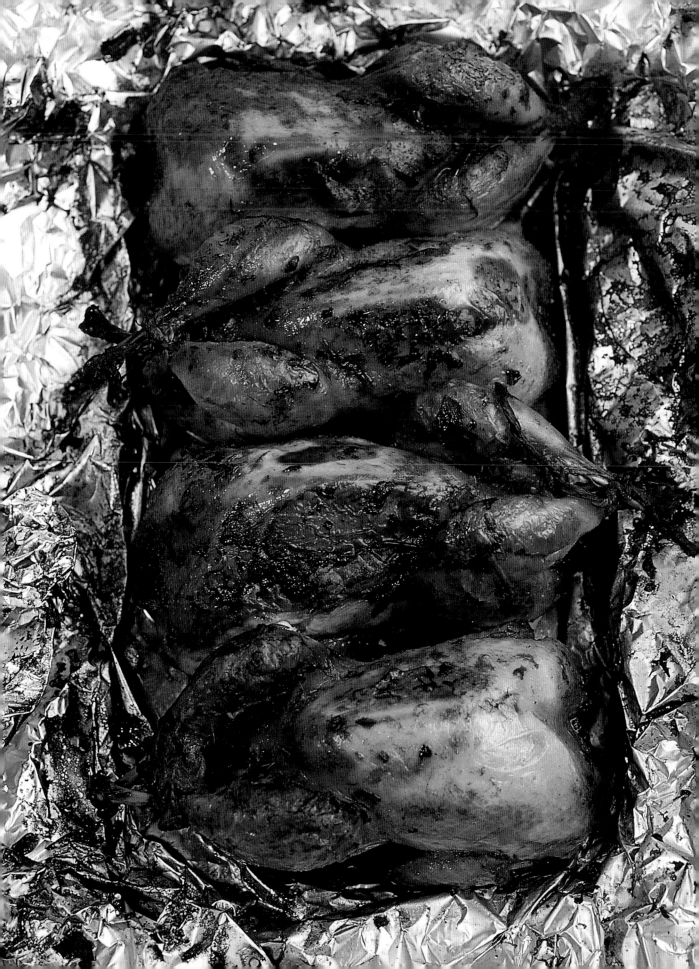

Chinese-style chicken wings

Without straying into soft-porn territory, I can't think of much that's nicer to nibble, suck and tease than a mahogany-glazed, sticky, slow-cooked chicken wing. Who can resist the way the succulent tidbits of flesh gently part from the twig-like bones or the sweet-savoury flavour? Well, *Sex in the City* Samantha may be greedier for king-size roosters, but then again she rarely eats anywhere other than bed.

ingredients for 2

12–16 chicken wings (depending on size)
rinsed and patted dry

FOR THE MARINADE

2 large garlic cloves
crushed and finely chopped

1 small 'thumb' of root ginger
peeled and grated

1 small onion
finely chopped

1 mild red chilli
de-seeded and finely chopped

2 tbsp dark soy sauce

2 tbsp oyster sauce

FOR THE DIPPING SAUCE

6 tbsp plum sauce

2 tbsp sweet chilli sauce

1 tbsp dark soy sauce

(optional) 1 tbsp rice vinegar

(to serve) lime or lemon wedges

Pile the chicken wings in a large non-reactive dish. Make the marinade by mixing all the ingredients together, then slather the wings thoroughly with it. Leave to marinate in a cool place for 2 to 24 hours – the longer the better.

Preheat the oven to 200°C fan/gas mark 7. Throw the chicken wings, complete with marinade, into a roasting tin (double-lined with foil if you don't want a lot of post-prandial scrubbing). Cook the wings for about 60 minutes, turning them occasionally and adding a splash of water to the pan each time.

Meanwhile, mix the dipping sauce ingredients together in a small bowl, adding rice vinegar to taste, if you like an extra tang. (It will keep for a few days in the fridge.)

Serve the chicken wings with the dip, a wedge of lime or lemon and a huge stack of paper napkins.

Lebanese chicken wings

The decor in most of London's Lebanese restaurants may be gilded and overlit, but the food is generally quite fantastic – simple, true and resoundingly well flavoured. I also love the fact that the repertoire of dishes remains steadfastly traditional and fashion-resistant. Lebanese-style chicken, whether it's wings, kebabs or quarters, is usually painted with a thick garlicky sludge, then chargrilled. It tastes sublime. Let the chicken mop up all the flavour from the marinade, but don't you start mopping it up with bread.

ingredients for 2

1 large whole head of garlic

3 tbsp olive oil

the juice of 1 lemon

12–16 chicken wings

Preheat the oven to 200°C fan/gas mark 7. Slice across the head of garlic to expose the tips of the cloves inside then wrap the whole head loosely in foil. Roast it for 30 minutes, or until the cloves are very soft. Squeeze the sweet, dark paste from each clove straight into a blender. Add the oil and whizz until smooth, then add the lemon juice.

Spread the chicken wings out in a close-fitting non-reactive dish. Pour over the garlic purée and massage it well into the wings. Leave the chicken to marinate for 24 to 48 hours in the fridge, turning it when you remember.

Preheat the oven to 200°C fan/gas mark 7 and bring the wings to room temperature before cooking them. Put them into a very roomy roasting tin, season and cook the wings for about 60 minutes, turning them halfway through and adding a splash of water to the pan occasionally. When they are gloriously brown and the meat is nearly falling off the bones, they are done. Serve with a pile of paper napkins for finger-wiping, and a big dish of tomato and onion salad.

more warm pitta bread is divine.

Skinny lamb chops + herb paste

My first mother-in-law (I've only had two) was not the world's greatest cook, nor did she have much money (but she was a terrific woman, I hasten to add). However, I did enjoy one meal that made a regular appearance. It was nothing more than lamb chops, cut so finely they were almost like bacon rashers – they weren't even English, but frozen New Zealand lamb – and then grilled almost to a cinder. I remember, with happiness, eating platefuls of them while we sat and watched television. Ah, the sophistication of Finchley in the Seventies. Nowadays I smother them in a pungent herb paste to add a bit more pizzazz, but the core notion of nibbling and teasing the meat off endless quantities of bones still holds true. So does the fact the lamb should be well charred – this is not an occasion for elegantly pink lamb.

ingredients for 2

2 garlic cloves
crushed and roughly chopped

1 shallot
roughly chopped

a handful of fresh basil

a handful of parsley

1 sprig of fresh rosemary
leaves roughly chopped

the zest of 1 lemon
and most of the juice

1 tsp smooth Dijon mustard

a little olive oil

750g very thinly cut lamb chops

Put all the ingredients, except the olive oil and lamb chops, into a blender or a mini food processor. Add some seasoning, then whizz everything coarsely. With the motor going, trickle in enough oil to make a thick sludge.

Put the lamb chops into a close-fitting non-reactive dish and smother them with the paste, massaging it in with your hands. Leave the chops to marinate in a cool place for 2 to 12 hours.

If you have a stonkingly good overhead grill, you can cook the lamb chops under that, but make sure the grill is thoroughly preheated. Grill the chops for 3–4 minutes each side, or until charred. Otherwise, very lightly oil a large cast-iron griddle or heavy frying pan and heat it over a medium-high flame. When it is very hot, put in the lamb chops in a single layer and cook them, undisturbed, for 3 minutes, then turn them and cook for a further 3–4 minutes, or until well browned.

Serve the chops piled up, with plenty of paper napkins for finger-wiping, and a big bowl of crunchy Greek-style salad.

Fiddly prawn and chilli salad

This is a recipe that Alastair Little, a splendid cook, devised in order to use up some leftover prawns after a photographic shoot for his seminal book, *Food of the Sun* (written with Richard Whittington). As with everything Alastair cooks, it is direct, unfussy and zipping with flavour. By the way, not all tiger prawns taste the same: the rust-coloured raw ones are better flavoured than the blue-black variety. And, if you can find scampi or langoustines, rather than tiger prawns, so very much the better. Unlikely though.

ingredients for 4

20–28 raw shell-on tiger prawns (depending on size)

the juice of 1 lemon

1 large red chilli
de-seeded and finely chopped

2 garlic cloves
crushed and finely chopped

a splash of extra-virgin olive oil

a small handful of parsley
leaves chopped

2 ripe tomatoes
blanched, de-seeded and finely chopped

1 red onion
finely chopped

(to serve) 8 lemon wedges

Without peeling them, 'butterfly' the prawns: cut down their length, belly-side, going nearly but not all the way through to the other side, then turn each prawn and press it firmly so it opens out. Arrange all the prawns, flesh-side up, on a large non-reactive dish. Squeeze lemon juice over the prawns, then scatter them with the chopped chilli and garlic. Season and splash them with a little olive oil. Leave the prawns to marinate in the fridge for 2 to 3 hours.

To cook the prawns, first heat a large cast-iron griddle over a high flame. Remove the prawns from the marinade (reserving it). When the pan is hot, arrange them in a single snug layer, shell-side down. Cook the prawns, undisturbed, for 5–6 minutes, basting them with any leftover marinade. When the flesh starts to turn opaque and shrinks away from the shells, they are done. (If you have to cook the prawns in batches, stop cooking them when they are still slightly translucent in the middle – then they won't toughen up while they are being kept warm.)

Arrange the prawns on a warm serving dish, strew them with the parsley, tomatoes and red onion, and season them. Serve the prawns at room temperature with wedges of lemon.

more douse with extra olive oil and serve hunks of French baguette to mop up the juices.

Cold lobster + coriander dipping sauce

When I die you will find 'lobster' (or 'crab') engraved on my heart, not 'Calais'. Anyway, the point is I adore them above all other foods, which is just as well as they are perfect for someone who is dieting.

A crucial factor in the success of the dipping sauce is that it must be made 'to taste' and that means your taste – not mine. Start off with the lesser amounts of chilli, sugar, lime juice, etc., and add more as required. The flavour should be resolutely vivid and pungent, but not so aggressive that it brings tears to your eyes.

ingredients for 2

2 (about 750g each) cooked native lobsters

FOR THE DIPPING SAUCE

2 large garlic cloves
finely chopped

1–2 mild green chillies
de-seeded and finely chopped

1–2 tbsp caster sugar

2–3 tbsp fresh lime juice

150–175ml Thai fish sauce (nam pla)

**2 tbsp tamarind sauce
(or pomegranate molasses)**

a handful of fresh coriander
leaves finely chopped

6–8 sprigs of fresh mint
leaves bundled up and finely sliced

Using a very heavy knife, split the lobsters in half down their backs from head to toe, then remove and discard the long, dark thread that runs down the length of the body meat. Discard the bony head parts, but the soft greenish-grey stuff that doesn't look very pretty is only the liver, and is perfectly edible. (I like it smeared on thick brown bread: any red matter is the roe and is very good beaten into a shellfish butter.) Tear off the claws and crack them open with a mallet (in a large plastic bag or under a damp tea towel). Remove the meat and pack it back into the shells.

To make the dipping sauce, combine the garlic, chilli, sugar and lime juice in a bowl. Whisk vigorously, then add the Thai fish sauce, tamarind and about 150ml of cold water, then whisk again. Taste, and adjust the flavours as desired, before adding the herbs.

Serve the lobsters with a variety of salads, and a bowl of dipping sauce each.

Lobster, crabs, prawns and the rest of the gang

It should be obvious that I am entirely devoted to shellfish in all its myriad forms. I don't care whether there's a mollusc, crustacean, bivalve or cephalopod on my plate, just as long as it's there in multiplicity.

I can't count how many happy hours I've spent loitering over a plate piled high with smoked prawns or little brown shrimps. What I also like about shellfish is that it can be approached as gregariously or selfishly as you want. While I am more than happy to tuck into a pint or two of prawns, solo and with quiet concentration, I am also delighted to sit round a table with a huge charger of shellfish beached in the middle and a group of friends to help demolish the contents. A typical fruits de mer, Suffolk-style, could include lobster, crab, oysters, slim razor clams, cooked mussels and cockles, brown shrimps and pink shrimps. Money and availability notwithstanding, it may also include big Mediterranean prawns. What I do refuse to countenance are whelks, on the grounds that the rubbery flesh would be better employed in dispersing an unruly rabble.

Another great thing, from a dietary point of view, is that while mayonnaise is the obvious partner, shellfish also lends itself very well to dressings founded on Thai flavours. The only thing I do miss is a bowl of thick hand-cut chips with my lobster. Nowadays I make do with Corn Thins, but I am not kidding either myself, or you, that it's quite the same thing.

Dealing with lobster

It's always a bit difficult to know just how far non-pros are prepared to go when it comes to preparing more esoteric food. I'm fairly confident that genuine cooks won't mind trimming up some kidneys or making a chicken stock, but not so sure that there is a great deal of enthusiasm out there for stabbing a live crab to death. The trouble is that home-cooked lobster is so much more gorgeous than lobster that's been lying on the fishmonger's slab for a couple of days. Naturally it's your decision whether to buy live or cooked lobster, but if it's the latter do make sure you buy it from a real fishmonger who is willing to pledge it has only just been dispatched. (And, please, it must be British, not one of those tasteless Canadian upstarts.) For more hardy cooks, here's how to kill and cook a lobster.

Put 3 handfuls of coarse sea salt in a huge saucepan (stockpot size), fill it with water and bring it to a boil. Pick up the (blue-black) live lobster by its midriff, with its claws still confined by rubber bands, and plunge it into the pot. It won't like it, but clamp the lid on the pan and within a few seconds it will be calm, i.e. dead. Bring the water back to a gentle boil, and cook the lobster for 15 minutes (this timing is for an ideal-sized 750g creature). Fish the (bright red) lobster out with tongs, put it in the sink and run cold water over it for 5 minutes. Leave the lobster to cool completely but preferably not in the fridge – unless it's a very hot day and it's not

going to be eaten for a while. (Refrigerating it will toughen up the flesh, but if you have to do it, then at least bring the lobster back to cool room temperature before serving it.)

Dealing with Crab

When it comes to killing crabs, I'm afraid I call on my friend Rod to do the dirty deed, but you probably won't have such an obliging (highly trained) chef-friend. I have to ask him because I simply cannot bring myself to take a sharpening steel and stab it straight into a lively crab. The reason for murdering a crab like this is that if you put it straight into boiling water it will normally shed its legs. If you don't have a Rod on hand,

order your crab from a reputable fishmonger who really will supply you with a freshly boiled creature, not one that's been hanging around.

Once the crab is dead it's not difficult to crack open. First, wrench off the legs and break them apart at the joints (discarding the pointed, furry feet). Put the claws and legs in a strong plastic bag or under a damp tea towel, and crack them with a meat mallet. Now turn the body upside down and pull off (and discard) the flap – or apron – that curls underneath the shell. (A wide, stubby apron signifies a female crab – more flavour – and a thin, longer apron, a male crab – more white meat.) Insert a short, sturdy knife in between the shell and the body of the crab, and twist the two sections apart. Pull off and discard the eye and mouth part, and the grey, feathered gills (also known as 'dead-man's fingers') which surround the dome of fine-shelled white body meat. Chop the body into quarters and, if you're preparing the crab for a *fruits de mer*, leave it like that. Otherwise, pick out all the white crab meat, cracking each little hollowed segment open as you go. The terracotta-brown meat can be used for dressed crab, or put in the freezer to be added to a sauce or stock at a later date.

Dealing with prawns

You will be pleased to hear that nine times out of ten, prawns are sold ready-cooked. This is simply because raw prawns decompose notoriously quickly. The only exception (and it's a relatively recent one) is tiger prawns which have been frozen and defrosted – so they're dead, if still raw. Whatever the size or colour, peeling a prawn involves the same simple process. First, pinch off the head, then pinch off the tail shell (although for some recipes, such as the Asian-spiced prawns on page 142, keep the tail on). Then peel off the body shell, attacking it from the belly-side and using the little legs to help you remove it. Don't discard all the debris but use it to make fabulous (and free) shellfish stock: freeze it in bags for later use.

Langoustines, which are the self-same thing as Dublin Bay prawns and scampi, are slightly different, having a craggy, hard shell and small lobster-like claws. Shell them as normal prawns, but if the claws are of reasonable size and you are enthusiastic, tear them off, crunch them with your teeth and suck out the meat.

Dealing with mussels and clams

Technically, you can eat mussels and clams while they are still alive but, as a victim of hepatitis A (acquired from a reputable seafood restaurant – heigh-ho – and I didn't sue) I wouldn't advise it. Before cooking mussels, give them a thorough scrub (although the rope-grown, farmed ones are much cleaner than wild mussels) and pull off the tufty beard which protrudes from between the shells. (This is what they use to attach themselves to boat bottoms, ropes and the like.)

Discard any very heavy mussels, which are likely to be sand-filled, and any that won't shut if you give them a sharp tap. Never feed live mussels with oatmeal, or any such nonsense, as they will suffocate. They will keep for 1–2 days in the bottom of the fridge, well wrapped in damp newspaper. Scrub clams, and discard any open ones, in just the same way as mussels.

To cook either type of bivalve, put a very large saucepan over a high flame and add suitable flavourings, such as wine, cider, shallots, onions, parsley, fennel – or not, depending on the recipe. Tip in the mussels or clams, cover the pot, and cook them for 3–4 minutes, shaking the pan vigorously from time to time. When the majority of the shells have opened, they are cooked. Discard any that remain closed.

TRUE or FALSE?

I am sitting at my desk looking at the outer packaging from two ready meals, both bought at the same leading supermarket. If anything proved what a con food labelling can be it's these. The first, which makes no claims for anything other than its succulence, tenderness and richness (oh, and the fact it's a new improved recipe – isn't it always) contains 85kcal per 100g and 1.1g of fat (of which 1.0g is saturated). The second packet is emblazoned with captions and symbols declaring it to contain less than 2% fat, and that it is 'healthy'. Let's just check on what that means exactly, shall we? Well, here's a surprise – the second packet contains exactly the same amount of fat, 1.1g, albeit only 0.2g of it is saturated (i.e. unhealthy) fat.

Okay, if you ate both meals in their entirety there would be a saving of 3.6g of saturated fat in the so-called healthy meal, but you would also be ingesting an extra 112kcal as well as 52g more carbohydrate (the amount of fibre is the same). Worryingly, there would also be 22g less protein in the so-called healthy meal. In other words, apart from a slight reduction in the level of saturated fat, the nutritional value of the 'healthy' meal is actually worse than the that of the normal meal. It may be legal for the producer to make such extravagant claims, but I am willing to bet my dog's headless plastic snowman that the average purchaser would expect something better from a meal that's trumpeted as 'healthy' compared to a casserole that makes no such claim.

What's irritating is that this type of disingenuous labelling and packaging is perfectly normal. Sweet biscuits are a prime case. Next time you're in a supermarket, examine the nutritional panel on a packet of, say, Café Noir (which I adore) and a packet of so-called slimmers' biscuits, and you'll find the former are probably less fattening. My advice is always to check the nutritional information panel on what you are buying, whatever the big writing on the front yells about fat content. And, don't fall for anything that shrieks, '88% fat free,' as if it were something laudable. Turn the statement back to front and you'll realise it means the food contains 12% fat – and that's a heck of a lot.

You should also be aware that most of the labelling concerning fat content has little legal basis. For example, while 'low-fat' means the product should contain less than 3g of fat per 100g, 'reduced fat' means nothing at all. Reduced from how much to how little? Your guess is as good as mine.

Truth no. 1 – low-fat (processed) food is often a complete con

While we're on the subject of buying food, I want to question the hoary old mandate that decrees you should never go shopping on a empty stomach. The philosophy behind this seems reasonable at first glance: a hungry person will pick up everything in sight and fill her trolley to the gunwales. Obviously this can't be a good thing. But hang on a minute. Isn't this presupposing that all your shopping is going to be fattening rubbish? What's wrong with a trolley laden with fresh fruit and vegetables, free-range poultry, meat and eggs? Nothing, of course. As my greatest eating lapses occur when the kitchen is empty of food, rather than full, I say that it's perfectly okay to go shopping when you have an appetite. Feeling a bit peckish (but not ravenous) as you wander round the supermarket is no bad thing and will encourage you to buy enough food to sustain you, healthily, for several days. On the other hand, if you're full up when you shop you won't buy enough. Then, when you can't find anything to eat you will grab whatever is going. Remember, if you are going to lose weight in the long term, the house must be filled with toothsome snacks, as well as the makings of a full-blown meal. So, go ahead and fill up that trolley.

Truth no. 2 – shopping on a full stomach means you won't buy enough food: shop when you are a bit hungry

If you haven't already noticed, food manufacturers have targeted fat as Enemy Number One. Well, yes and no: it's certainly not the whole story. Without getting too hung up on the current fashion for multiple food allergies, I think I have more problem with carbohydrate than I do with fat. So, although I don't think it's a good idea to eliminate any food group totally, I favour a high-ish protein, low-ish carbohydrate regime, which means I can still have the odd bowl of fibre-rich porridge, as well as bananas. There is some scientific truth to my belief. Apparently, ingestion of proteins maximises the effect of appetite-deadening serotonin – in other words, protein makes us feel more satisfied. Proteins also burn up more calories (about twice as many during the two-hour period after eating) because our bodies have to work much harder at breaking them down than carbohydrates. In a recent trial, involving 50 fat women, those on a low-carb diet lost 10 pounds more weight than those on a low-fat diet.

But there really are no magic combinations of foods – and no wonder solutions. As I've already said, if you take in more calories than you use, you will put on weight. If you take in fewer, you will lose weight. Any diet that delivers this equation will work, whether it's a high-fat, high-protein, high-carbohydrate or high-fibre diet. Even an exclusive diet of Smarties will succeed if you eat less than 1200kcal worth of them a day – you'll be a very acned corpse, but there you go. It's simply that faddish diets are not sustainable over a period of time. For a start they can be positively dangerous and, for the average person, they are completely unrealistic in their demands. I repeat, you have to find your own diet, one that works for you, not for someone else. But I also believe that a varied diet is more likely to see you through – albeit one that favours protein, veg and fruit, and goes easy on the fat and carbohydrate.

Truth no. 3 – fat is not the only enemy

Yet another adage that I refute is the one that tells you it's a bad thing to weigh yourself every day. The authors of this statement must be able to eat anything they like with impunity, or they wouldn't say something so ridiculous. They certainly can't share my ability to put on 5 pounds between Monday and Wednesday – or 8 pounds in a week. I am not exaggerating, as I know many other fatties will bear witness. It is simply terrifying how easily I can load on the pounds. On occasion it has got to the point where I have avoided going on holiday to places where I know the food is too good, because I will eat too much of it. In the middle of my big weight-loss year we were meant to go to Italy for a week, but we went to Denmark instead, a decision that didn't exactly thrill my husband. But I knew that there the food would not be an overriding factor. (Also, the Danes are big on fish and shellfish, and it's not difficult to leave the thin slice of bread that underpins their gorgeous traditional open sandwiches.)

Far from avoiding the scales, I treat them like a close friend (or at least a pet crocodile) and weigh myself every morning without fail. You could call this obsessive behaviour, but I maintain it's a sensible precaution. Yes, of course one's weight can fluctuate a little, but that needle gives a pretty damned good idea which way the cookie is crumbling. If I know I have not been quite as conscientious in my eating pattern as I might have been, the scales will soon show it. Far better that I get a gentle nudge when not too much damage has been done, than wait a week and find that I am half a stone heavier. On a recent trip to Venice (where I eat as prodigiously as I walk) I was positively thrilled to find a set of scales in our hotel bathroom so I could keep an eye on things. The only caveat is that it really is worth investing in a decent set – the type where you can't subtract a few pounds by favouring one leg or the other.

Truth no. 4 – weighing yourself every day is not a hindrance

You will find my thoughts about exercise, and whether it's really necessary, in a later chapter. Briefly, I disagree with those pundits who maintain it's the only way to lose weight. In fact, I am living proof that it simply isn't true. But I do think it can be very good for your ego, and as you get older it makes a lot of sense to stay fit and supple. By all means include some exercise, either formal or ad hoc, but don't think it will solve any problems by itself.

Truth no. 5 – you do not have to exercise to lose weight

I've already said what I feel about breakfast in Working Woman's Reality, but I think it's worth repeating that some of us simply don't want or can't stomach food early in the day. I have heard and understood all the stuff about one's stomach being at its most efficient before 9.00 am, but God forgot to prime my own organ to accept sustenance at an early hour. If I do try to eat soon after I've woken up, I don't feel revived, I feel nauseous. I've also 'wasted' a considerable part of my daily calorie ration on a meal I don't want. I would far rather save the calories for later in the day, when they mean something to me. If this means I am eating badly, so be it. Remember, I still managed to lose four stone.

Truth no. 6 – eating breakfast is not imperative

To sum up, here's a universal truth:

To diet successfully you must find your own truths

beyond
BAKED BEANS

I was in a real quandary as to what to call this chapter. Dinner parties have long ceased to exist in the format I remember as a young adult. The very mention of the words 'dinner' and 'party' in tandem excites the sort of mockery and derision from my peers that used to be levelled at people who had a flight of plaster ducks on the sitting room wall. I can quite understand why. Those awful, endless days of shopping and preparation; the time that went into buying flowers, candles and esoteric aperitifs, not to mention Bendicks Bittermints and bottles of Bardolino; the laborious task of setting and decorating the table; and the multiplicity of puddings that had to be offered – Escoffier himself would have been daunted by the dogged expertise that went into making the myriad cream-puffed confections. By the time the evening arrived (always Saturday, of course) and everything was ready, the hostess (I use the gender advisedly) was ready too – for bed.

Naturally, I was that woman, and I am delighted the nonsense has stopped. Now it's as normal to meet friends in a restaurant as to invite them round to one's house. In fact, the very concept of entertaining has utterly altered – even the word is anathema. It's not so much to do with offering hospitality any more (or, heaven forbid, trying to impress people) as wanting to share space and time, as well as food and wine, with people you really like. Dinner is now supper, and supper is more likely to be eaten in the kitchen than the dining room.

But, despite my relief that times have changed, I still make a bit more effort when the meal is for people other than my immediate family. I hope I don't go over the top (I can hear my husband saying, "Of course you do, don't be bloody stupid"), I just haven't got the nerve to serve scrambled eggs to someone I've invited a month in advance and who has driven 50 miles to see us – well, not unless the eggs are liberally strewn with white truffles. So, you won't get a frozen pizza if you come to my house for dinner, but neither will I put myself in hock, either mentally or physically, to get a decent meal on the table. Which brings me back to the question: what do we now call the kind of food that requires a bit more effort than tuna fish salad (however nice) but less than tournedos Rossini? Your guess is as good as mine.

Oddly enough, if you do decide to go out for a meal you may well find it easier to stick to your diet. I've never eaten better in restaurants than when I've given the chef a free hand to make me something unfattening out of the available ingredients. It's a bit like pre-ordering a Buddhist vegetarian meal when you're flying: without question, yours will be the freshest, most interesting food on the plane. In my diet diary, I still have the details of one particular restaurant meal: after a starter of smoked salmon with an Asian-style cucumber salad I was given a fabulous (off-menu) main course of chunky poached cod with wild asparagus and a light fresh tomato and caper dressing. I am not suggesting you cause a great fuss (as a restaurateur who is allergic to people with allergies, that would be hypocritical), but a commercial kitchen will always have a plethora of ingredients that can be served simply.

Although it's unlikely you need to be reminded, it is still worth mentioning that most Indian, Mexican and Chinese food is outrageously high in calories. Conversely, Japanese, Vietnamese and Thai food is fairly safe, if you remember to avoid fried foods and peanut sauces. Regional Italian food is reasonably kind to dieters, as long as you don't wade into the pasta or risotto. But, of course, the real villain in any cuisine is likely to be oil, whatever its provenance – olive, argan, walnut or pumpkin seed. It's a fashion thing, but most chefs nowadays have a fetish for finishing off dishes with a flourish of oil, particularly salads, bread, fish and anything griddled. Just one innocuous-looking swish of green-gold lubricant – one that isn't mentioned on the menu and you haven't asked for – can account for 500kcal. I always ask the waiter to hold the oil and/or butter when I am ordering, as it can make a heck of a difference.

Another good thing about eating out is that there won't be any leftovers. Think about it. It's not difficult playing the diet heroine while you're being watched, but what happens when everyone has gone home and you're clearing up? Who scoffs the last tranche of apple tart? Or the next day, when the remnants of the lemon meringue pie are waving at you from the fridge – how strong will your resolve be then? It's not just dessert that's easier to resist in a restaurant, it's the whole deal, starting with alcohol. At home, in the happy company of friends, it takes quite a bit of willpower to spurn the glass of wine that your partner is just about to pour in your glass. But it's a doddle if you're eating out, because all you have to do is offer to be the driver. In a trice you have abrogated all responsibility and allowed the law to take over.

You can dismiss the waiter in a restaurant, too. I don't mean in an unfriendly, P45 kind of way, but when he or she offers you the bread it's very quick and painless to say, "No, thank you," and off the basket goes. At home, the bread basket sits in the middle of the table for the entire meal, along with the butter. At some point you will probably find your hand straying towards it (or, in my case, certainly straying towards it). The same is true of chocolates: when my slim friends refuse the L'Artisan du Chocolat salted caramels or Charbonnel et Walker rose and violet creams I so thoughtfully provide (as they always do – that's why they are slim) do I pack them up and put them away for another occasion? Do I hell.

However, if I do decide to have friends round for dinner, I don't punish them with a meal that appears excessively dietary. Admittedly, it's a damned sight easier in summer, when you can put a beautiful sea bass on the barbie or throw together a fabulous *fruits de mer*. But then dieting in general is much less difficult in the summer when there's such a profusion of fruit, and even radishes are a delight to eat (with a dish of crystalline sea salt).

Whatever the season, the main danger for the non-dieter lies on the fringes of the meal, e.g. the pre-prandial nuts, olives, warm nibbles, bread and butter, glass of wine, and the chocolates or biscuits that accompany the coffee. If you can avoid those, and the dessert, you're home and dry.

All the recipes that follow are pretty low in calories, but I've also indicated at the bottom of many of them where the guests can have a bit extra or the dieter needs to hold back. At this point I am tempted to say 'enjoy', but as that's an expression that makes me want to punch the utterer in the teeth, I won't. (How often have you been invited by a waiter to enjoy your meal when being seated at a restaurant table? I am quite proud that – up to now – I have neither grimaced nor said out loud, "Well, that's rather up to you, mate.") Instead, I will express the earnest wish that you find these recipes inviting, enjoyable to cook and toothsome – and that any movement on the scales is to the left.

A BIGGER SPLASH

Like the curate's egg, I know it's impossible to be partly virginal but I think the inclusion of one teaspoon of dry sherry per glass of tomato juice in a **Nearly Virgin Mary** hardly constitutes an alcoholic misdemeanour of the first water. **Spritz** (not to be confused with Spritzer) hails from Venice and is commonly drunk in the neighbourhood bars: with its bitter stab, a Spritz can stir the most jaded of taste buds. Use an everyday dry white wine, perhaps a Sauvignon Blanc or Pinot Grigio. **Bellini** is the house drink at Harry's Bar (again in Venice) and, while I realise it's unlikely you will be whizzing up your own fresh white peach juice (although it's not impossible), at least use best-quality frozen peach purée rather than the bottled stuff: yellow peach juice isn't to be considered. **Bucks Fizz** is the evergreen combination of orange juice and champagne. Again, using genuine, freshly squeezed OJ – the type that starts with just-cut oranges – makes all the difference. The reason I suggest these two particular cocktails is that you can bump up the juice content at the expense of the alcohol, and still be left with something festive and flirty to drink.

Nearly Virgin Mary Combine 1 litre of tomato juice (I like Sainsbury's own-brand long-life juice, in cartons), a few dashes of Tabasco sauce, a few dashes of Worcestershire sauce, a good squeeze of lemon juice, a pinch of fine sea salt and a few grindings of black pepper and 4 teaspoons of dry sherry. Whisk together, adjust the seasonings to taste, then serve over ice in tall tumblers. I always drink tomato juice with a fat straw because I don't like the way the ice bumps into my teeth. It's up to you. Serves 4.

Spritz Combine 75ml Campari and 75ml ice-cold dry white wine in a chilled wine glass or tumbler. Splash in 50ml ice-cold soda water and stir. Serves 1.

Bellini Pour 50ml good-quality Prosecco (Italian sparkling wine) into a champagne glass, then gently add 125ml white peach purée and stir with a long-handled spoon. (At Harry's Bar they display a rather marvellous inverted snobbery by serving this truly beautiful aperitif in a nothingy little wine glass.) Serves 1.

Bucks Fizz Pour 50ml dry champagne into a champagne glass then gently add 125ml freshly squeezed orange juice. (Do it the other way round and it will all fizz over the top in an alarming fashion, making a horrible mess.) Serves 1.

STARTERS

Cantaloupe and crab salad + ginger dressing

There is something almost mystically right about the combination of seafood and ginger, melon and seafood, or ginger and melon. The zippy, fresh flavours conspire in perfect harmony. If fresh crab is hard to come by (and canned really won't do), use Greenland prawns instead – whole ones that you peel yourself.

ingredients for 6

the zest and juice of 3 lemons

1 garlic clove
crushed and roughly chopped

1 'thumb' of root ginger
peeled and roughly chopped

1 stick of lemon grass
roughly sliced

2 tbsp not-cheap honey

6 tbsp olive oil

FOR THE SALAD

2 cantaloupe (or Charentais) melons
de-seeded and rind removed

½ cucumber
halved lengthways and de-seeded

2 tbsp chopped chives

a small handful of parsley
leaves roughly chopped

350g fresh white crabmeat

(to serve) a few sprigs of watercress

To make the dressing, put all the ingredients, except the olive oil, into a small saucepan set over a high flame. Bring to a boil and carry on boiling, uncovered, until the liquid has reduced by about half. Press the contents through a sieve, discarding the debris, then season the liquid and leave it to cool. Whisk in the olive oil, taste, and adjust the seasoning if necessary. Leave the dressing to one side. (It will keep, refrigerated, for 2 to 3 days.)

Cut the melon into bite-sized chunks. Cut the cucumber into fairly thin slices. Put the melon, cucumber and herbs into a large bowl and toss them together. Pour over the dressing and toss again. Distribute the melon mixture between the serving plates, encouraging any excess dressing to drip back into the bowl. Add the crab to the remaining dressing – there won't be much, and that's okay – toss it gently, then spoon it on top of the salad. Finish with a sprig of watercress and serve immediately

Asian-spiced prawns

Another Alastair, this time Hendy, writes very persuasive recipes – often Asian-inspired and always beautifully styled and photographed. His way of cooking tiger prawns has proved a great hit on our menu at the Crown and Castle, especially on Saturday night – although we haven't been asked to serve a pint of lager with the fiery succulent prawns... yet. I've had to adapt the recipe, partly because he deserves better copy editors (two mistakes in one recipe is going it a bit) and partly to suit our own taste. We also like to serve the prawns with a drizzle of coriander-whizzed natural yoghurt and some crunchy Asian-style salad: make it with finely sliced carrot, cucumber, red onion (or red pepper) and coriander leaves, then toss it in rice wine vinegar, palm sugar and chilli dressing, flavoured with a little ground cumin and/or coriander.

ingredients for 4

2 tbsp dried chilli flakes

1 heaped tsp black peppercorns

2 tsp cumin seeds

1 whole star anise

3 tbsp groundnut (or vegetable) oil

1 tbsp fenugreek seeds

4 (or 2 banana) shallots
roughly chopped

5 garlic cloves
roughly chopped

2–3 pinches of ground turmeric

(optional) a small handful of fresh curry leaves

24 raw shell-on tiger prawns
heads and shells removed (but not the tails) and de-veined

Heat a small heavy frying pan over a medium flame. When it's hot, put in the chilli, peppercorns, cumin seeds and star anise. Dry-fry for 1 minute, stirring, then tip the spices into a mortar and grind them finely (or whizz in a small grinder). Set aside. Heat 1 tablespoon of oil in the same frying pan and add the fenugreek. Stir until the seeds start crackling, then remove the pan and leave it to cool.

Put the shallots, garlic, turmeric and remaining oil into a liquidiser and add all the ground spices, including the fenugreek and its oil, some salt and the curry leaves (if using). Whizz to a coarse paste.

Put the prawns in a non-reactive dish and slather them with the paste. Leave them to marinate in a cool place for 2 hours. You can now thread them on to (soaked) wooden skewers – if you like needless work – or you can cook them free-form. Heat a large heavy frying pan over a medium-high flame and, when it's hot, put in the prawns in a single layer. Cook them in batches, if necessary. Grill the prawns for 4–6 minutes, turning them halfway through. Serve immediately.

Smoked eel, cucumber and radish salad

Although most good fishmongers (the few that remain) sell smoked eel, not too many supermarkets stock it. I find the quality very variable, but when it's good, it's wonderful stuff – hence the high price. Order it from a specialist mail order company, or substitute smoked salmon. You could also replace the full-fat crème fraîche with a low-fat version: I prefer less of the real thing, but it's up to you. I have Lorna Wing, a very stylish woman, to thank for this equally stylish salad.

ingredients for 4

2 tbsp crème fraîche

1 tbsp creamed horseradish

2 tbsp finely chopped dill

115g smoked eel fillets
cut into fine strips

½ cucumber
halved lengthways, de-seeded and
cut into 'matchsticks'

**a handful of radishes
(preferably French Breakfast)**
trimmed, sliced and cut
into 'matchsticks'

**(to serve) 4 handfuls of trimmed
watercress**

Mix the crème fraîche, horseradish and dill together in the bottom of a large bowl. Add the smoked eel, cucumber and radish, reserving a little of the veg for the garnish (hate that word, but find me another). Gently toss everything together until thoroughly combined, but not mushy.

Mentally divide the mixture into 4. Place an 8cm biscuit cutter into the centre of a serving plate and lightly press in enough of the mixture to fill it. Smooth the surface with the back of a spoon, then carefully lift away the cutter. Wipe the cutter clean before carrying on with the rest of the mixture.

Toss the watercress with the reserved cucumber and radish and plump a little clump on to each plate. Serve immediately.

more be very English (no, I don't mean British) and serve the smoked eel salad with thinly sliced brown bread and butter, the crusts removed.
less how does a Krisproll sound?

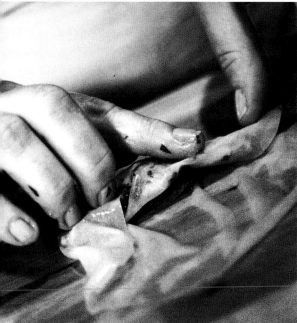

Vietnamese rice paper rolls

Purists will recognise that pomegranate molasses has no place in Vietnamese cooking. Tough. I have huge reservations about fusion food, but this is one instance where the sweet-sourish note struck by the (Middle Eastern) molasses adds to rather than detracts from an otherwise classic recipe – classic, if you're prepared to overlook the Chinese plum sauce as well. If you prefer, use small wafer-thin strips of rare lean steak rather than the prawns.

ingredients for 4

1 (50g) packet of rice flour pancakes

300g prawns (peeled weight)

1 shallot
very finely chopped

the zest of 1 lime and 2 tsp lime juice
zest very finely chopped

1 tbsp each of chopped fresh mint, coriander and flat leaf parsley

2 tbsp pomegranate molasses

2 tbsp rice (or cider) vinegar

½ cucumber
cut lengthways, de-seeded
and chopped into tiny dice

½ small red pepper
de-seeded and cut into tiny dice

FOR THE SAUCE

½ (320g) bottle of Sharwood's plum sauce

about 1 tbsp chilli sauce

Moisten the pancakes as instructed on the packet – or dip one briefly into warm water, wet your hands and gently stroke both sides until the pancake is soft and pliable but not squidgy. Repeat with the other pancakes – you will need 8 in total – covering them with clingfilm as you go to prevent them drying out.

Combine all the other ingredients in a large bowl, and season. Put a teaspoon of the mixture on one edge of a pancake and make one tight roll. Run a line of mixture on top of it, fold the sides in and continue rolling to make a cylindrical parcel. (The filling should show through.) Refrigerate the rolls for a maximum of 3 hours, clingfilmed.

Mix the plum and chilli sauces together. Taste, and adjust the quantities as desired, then serve with the rolls.

less don't wrap the mixture in pancakes (which may be as well if you live in the sticks, far from an Oriental food shop) but pile the salad into Little Gem or Cos leaves instead.

Seared beef carpaccio + mustard sauce

Carpaccio was invented at Harry's Bar in Venice to honour the eponymous Venetian painter and his characteristic blood-red palette. At 35 quid a plate, the profits from this one dish could restore the whole city and still leave change for the vaporetto. I know the setting is not quite so extraordinary in Orford, where we have our hotel, the Crown and Castle, but nor is the £7.50 that we charge for our own rendition. And you could say ours was better as we only use properly hung fillet of beef. Real carpaccio is completely raw but I like the fillet seared first, as it adds extra contrast in both colour and flavour. Omit this stage, if you prefer, but still chill the beef before slicing it.

ingredients for 6

a drop of olive oil

about 600g beef fillet (in one piece)
very well trimmed

(to serve) wild rocket

FOR THE MUSTARD SAUCE

1 tbsp smooth Dijon mustard

1 tsp unrefined caster sugar

1 tbsp red wine vinegar

2 tbsp groundnut (or vegetable) oil

75ml whipping cream

Heat a heavy frying pan over a high flame. Very lightly oil the beef and season it. When the pan is blazing-hot, put in the fillet and quickly colour it all over. Remove the beef and chill it on ice for a few minutes, then chuck the ice and refrigerate for a few hours or up to 3 days.

Slice the chilled beef thinly. Lay 2 or 3 slices on a piece of clingfilm, cover them with another layer of clingfilm, then use a rolling pin to bash and/or roll the beef out until it's paper-thin. Remove the top layer of clingfilm and turn the slices on to one of the serving plates, covering it completely. Repeat with the remaining beef.

To make the sauce, whisk the mustard, sugar, vinegar and seasoning together, then whisk in the oil and cream.

Season the carpaccio, then trickle on the mustard sauce in fine lines, and serve with a handful of rocket.

more strew Parmesan shavings over the carpaccio.
less the carpaccio still tastes good with only a little of the sauce (and no Parmesan).

Jambon persillé

This glistening terrine of pink moist ham set in a tarragon-flavoured jelly, madly speckled with bright green parsley, is a traditional Burgundian dish. It's not hard to see why it's often served at village festivities, particularly at Easter time, because it keeps well, is easy to make in large quantities and looks spectacular. The only fly in the ointment, for a British palate, is the jelly factor. We've become very squeamish about texture over the last few decades (viz. the closure of so many eel and pie shops), but I am old enough to adore it, whether savoury or sweet. Either serve the terrine straight from the bowl – as they do in Parisian brasseries – or turn it out. There's quite a lot of work involved but all of it can (indeed, should) be done ahead.

The usual sauce to serve with jambon persillé is a thin mayonnaise flavoured with mustard. But you could also add chopped herbs, such as tarragon, parsley, chervil or chives. Other traditional accompaniments are toasted sourdough or country bread spread with slabs of unsalted butter (not so good for the dieter) and small gherkins or cornichons (perfect for the dieter).

ingredients for 6+

1.25kg raw unsmoked bacon shoulder

a pinch of black peppercorns

a pinch of juniper berries

1 celery stick

2 shallots

1 fresh or dried bay leaf

5 bushy sprigs of fresh tarragon

a small handful of parsley

1 (75cl) bottle of dry white wine

FOR THE JELLY

6 gelatine leaves

3 tbsp tarragon (or white wine) vinegar

2 large handfuls of flat leaf parsley
leaves roughly chopped

2 bushy sprigs of fresh tarragon
leaves roughly chopped

FOR THE SAUCE

225ml home-made or good-quality mayonnaise

1 tbsp tarragon (or white wine) vinegar

1 tbsp smooth Dijon mustard

2 tbsp whipping cream

1 tbsp salted capers
rinsed and roughly chopped

Cut the bacon into 8–10 cm chunks, rind and all. Put them in a large saucepan and cover with cold water. Bring the bacon to a boil over a medium heat, uncovered, then reduce the heat and gently simmer for 10 minutes. Drain the bacon and rinse it under cold running water to remove the scum.

Wash out the saucepan, put the bacon back in and tuck in all the spices, vegetables and herbs. Pour in the wine and top up with just enough cold water to cover. Put the pan over a medium flame and again bring to a simmer, uncovered. Immediately reduce the heat so only the odd bubble rises to the surface – no livelier, or the stock will go cloudy and ruin the jelly. Poach gently for about 90 minutes, or until the bacon is tender.

Carefully pour the contents of the pan through a damp muslin-lined colander, reserving the stock. Put the bacon in a bowl to cool with a clean damp cloth over the top. Pour about 600ml of the stock into a pan and keep it hot. (Use the rest to make lentil soup.) When the bacon is cool enough to handle, cut it into small cubes, discarding the rind and any very ugly bits of fat – but leave a little bit of fat for texture.

To make the jelly, put the gelatine leaves into a bowl, cover them with cold water and leave them to soak for 5 minutes, or until they are soft and squidgy. Scoop out the leaves, squeeze off the surplus water, then whisk them into the hot stock. When they have completely dissolved, set the stock aside in a cool place until it begins to jellify. Stir in the vinegar and all but 1 tablespoon each of the chopped parsley and tarragon. Add the bacon and plenty of pepper (but no salt). Tip the mixture into a 1.5 litre serving bowl or terrine and tamp down any bits that poke up. Cover the dish with clingfilm and refrigerate it for at least 8 hours, or until the jelly has set quite firmly.

For the sauce, mix all the ingredients together, adding the reserved parsley and tarragon. It should be thick but pourable, so add a little skimmed milk or water if it's too stiff. Taste and adjust the seasoning, adding more mustard or vinegar if required.

If you decide to turn the jambon persillé out, dip the bowl into very hot water for about 15 seconds to melt the surface of the jelly. Either way, cut the jambon persillé into thick wedges and serve with the sauce spooned over.

more the accompaniments mentioned in the introduction are essential – and a basket filled with hunks of French baguette...
less... but not so essential you have to eat them.

Grilled red pepper and chicory salad + shaved Parmesan

Here's a good way of using those beguiling pointy red peppers (variously called Extra Sweet, Sweet Long or Sweet Mediterranean Pointed Peppers) that look like pigs' pizzles – or, if you prefer, cute little elves' hats. That much-vaunted sweetness is offset perfectly by the slightly bitter flavour of the chicory. With a dribble of dusky balsamic vinegar and some nutty shards of Parmesan, the flavours add up to a harmonious whole. (To make long fine shavings, use a potato peeler to sweep down the wedge of Parmesan.)

ingredients for 4

4 pointed red peppers
halved lengthways, including the stalks, and de-seeded

2 heads of white Belgian chicory
trimmed and quartered lengthways, leaving a little root still attached

a little extra-virgin olive oil

1–2 tbsp balsamic vinegar

a good handful of Parmesan shavings

Preheat the grill. Arrange the halved peppers in a grill pan (or on a heavy baking tray), skin-side down, then stuff each half with a wedge of chicory. Trace the peppers with olive oil and season them.

Position the grill pan about a hand's length away from the elements and grill the peppers for 6–8 minutes, or until they are frazzled at the edges and the chicory is golden-tinged. Remove the tray and immediately dribble a few drops of balsamic vinegar over the chicory – don't go mad, because it's very intense and quite horrible when used too lavishly. Divide the peppers among 4 serving plates and strew Parmesan shavings over the top. Serve while still warm.

more be more lavish with the oil and Parmesan, and serve with a basket of ciabatta to mop up the juices.
less there's so much flavour, you only need a trace of oil and a feathering of Parmesan.

Griddled leek and feta salad

I love both leek and lentil salads but I am not sure that my fellow countrymen share my enthusiasm – this type of salad tends to go down better in France, I think. I am also more than happy to eat warm leeks plainly dressed with vinaigrette rather than tarted up with sharp cheese (as in this recipe). Don't dismiss the capers when you spot them in the ingredients list: salted capers are much less astringent than those packed in vinegar, and add a thrilling verdant kick.

ingredients for 4

1 tbsp tarragon (or cider) vinegar

1 tsp tarragon (or mild German) mustard

100ml fruity extra-virgin olive oil

FOR THE SALAD

**about 1kg slim leeks
(no thicker than copper piping)**
the pale green and white part only and roots trimmed

1 tbsp extra-virgin olive oil

a large handful of flat leaf parsley
leaves chopped

4 bushy sprigs of fresh tarragon
leaves chopped

100g real Greek or Cypriot feta cheese
roughly crumbled

2 tbsp salted capers
rinsed and drained

To make the dressing, whisk the vinegar and mustard together with some seasoning, then whisk in the olive oil to make a thick emulsion. Leave to one side.

Slice the leeks in half lengthways but not all the way through – they should remain intact. Wash them thoroughly under cold running water. Bring a large saucepan of salted water to a boil over a high flame and cook the leeks for about 5 minutes, uncovered, or until they are just tender. Drain thoroughly, then lay the leeks on a clean tea towel, pat them as dry as you can with kitchen paper, and nudge them back into shape.

Place a cast-iron griddle over a high flame. Very lightly oil the leeks, then lay them diagonally on the griddle (in 2 batches, if necessary). Cook them for about 2 minutes on each side, or until nicely marked. Transfer them to a serving dish, season generously and souse with the dressing. Turn the leeks and strew them with the chopped herbs, crumbled feta and capers. Serve at warm room temperature.

more be as lavish as you like with the dressing and serve the leeks with French bread or focaccia.
less go easy on both dressing and feta, and forgo the bread.

Smoked ham + Thai melon salad

I have Henry Harris to thank for this inspired combination, which is a real hit whenever I serve it. Henry, like all good chefs, really loves eating, and knows when and how to keep things simple. This is merely an Asian-style rendition of the classic Parma ham and melon combination, but is possibly even better. (It also works very well with fresh mangoes and, in the depths of winter, they are a much better bet than lacklustre melons.) I've slightly readjusted the proportions of the original recipe to suit my own taste and you must feel free to do the same, depending on how chilli-hot, savoury or sweetish you'd like the dressing to be. (It will keep for a few days, refrigerated, and is as good with chicken or shellfish as it is with the melon.)

ingredients for 4

1 Thai chilli
de-seeded and finely chopped

1 'thumb' of root ginger (or galangal)
peeled and finely grated

1 stick of lemon grass
a single inner leaf only, very finely chopped

6 tbsp Thai fish sauce (nam pla)

a small handful of fresh coriander
leaves chopped

1–3 tsp unrefined caster sugar

the juice of 1 lime

**2 ripe cantaloupe melons
(or small Charentais)**
peeled, de-seeded and cut into thin slices

**8–12 thin slices of Parma ham (or
speck, coppa or Black Forest ham)**

Mix together the chilli, ginger, lemon grass, fish sauce and coriander. Add 1 teaspoon of sugar and half the lime juice, then taste the dressing. Add more sugar and/or lime juice, as desired: the dressing should be tangy and lively, but not so acidic it bites your head off.

Divvy the melon among four serving plates (as simple, plain and Asian-looking as possible). Pour over enough dressing to season rather than drown the melon, then arrange furls of ham to the side. Serve immediately.

Buffalo mozzarella + Comice pears

Of course you can make this with any kind of pear, but you'd be a fool. Doyenné du Comice, to give these aromatic, richly flavoured pears their full moniker, are so outstanding compared to most other varieties. The only caveat (and it applies to all pears) is that you must buy them when they are still hard and bring them home to ripen gently in the warmth of the kitchen.

It also matters that you buy the freshest mozzarella. Buffalo milk mozzarella (mozzarella di bufala) has far more character than the more ubiquitous cow's-milk version, and is even better if you can find it sold loose in a bowl, drowned in whey. Supermarket buffalo mozzarella tends to come in smaller balls than the type sold loose, hence the uncertainty about how much you will need.

The combination of the tender, yoghurty mozzarella with the luscious pears is simple and joyous. A trickle of fruity extra-virgin olive oil and a grinding of black pepper are all that's needed to make this one of my favourite food collaborations.

ingredients for 4

3–4 balls of fresh buffalo mozzarella
drained

3 ripe Comice pears
peeled, cored and quartered

a little fruity extra-virgin olive oil

(to serve) a handful or two of rocket

Either slice the mozzarella thickly or, better still, tear it roughly into large, shaggy shards. Divide the mozzarella and pears among 4 serving plates, arranging the elements as you will: I like a careless, exuberant, rustic look. Season with lots of black pepper and a smidgen of fine sea salt, then trickle on the oil.

The distinct lack of colour doesn't worry me in the slightest, but if you can't bear the pallor of white mozzarella, ivory pears and brassy olive oil, thrust a small bunch of rocket on to each plate. Eat immediately.

more be more lavish with the olive oil and offer hunks of sourdough bread to wipe the plates clean.
less go very gently with the oil.

MAIN COURSES

Ruddy fish stew

You would hardly know that we had a culture of fish stew in this country so often do you hear about bouillabaisse and so rarely about cullen skink or partan bree. This delightfully messy recipe (to eat, that is) has a great flavour and a horribly long list of ingredients, mitigated by the fact that all the cooking – except the fish – can be done the day before. The eating is certainly worth the fuss of the preparation.

ingredients for 6

2 tbsp olive oil

1 large Spanish onion
finely chopped

1 celery stalk
finely chopped

2 medium carrots
finely chopped

4 garlic cloves
crushed and chopped

1 mild red chilli
de-seeded and finely chopped

2 good pinches of paprika

1 pinch of saffron threads

about 250g tomato passata

2 bushy sprigs of fresh oregano and/or thyme

350ml fruity red wine

1 litre fish stock or water

24 smallish live clams
rinsed and any open clams discarded

1.5kg live mussels
well rinsed, beards removed and any open mussels discarded

600g red mullet or snapper fillets
cut into small skin-on escalopes

18 raw shell-on tiger prawns

a handful of fresh basil
leaves torn

a handful of fresh parsley
leaves roughly chopped

Heat the oil in a very large saucepan over a low-medium flame. Add the onion, celery and carrots, and cook gently for 15 minutes, or until softened, stirring occasionally. Add the garlic, chilli, paprika and saffron, and continue to cook for 2 minutes. Raise the heat and add the passata, oregano, wine and stock. Bring the broth to a boil, then reduce the heat, cover and simmer gently for 40 minutes.

Meanwhile, cook the clams and mussels. Put another very large saucepan over a high flame and, when it is hot, tip in the clams and cook them, covered, for 1 minute. Add the mussels and continue to cook, still covered, for another 2–3 minutes, shaking the pan once or twice. When the shells have opened, remove the pan from the heat. Scoop out the shellfish and strain the juices through a damp muslin-lined sieve, reserving them. Discard any closed mussels or clams.

Pick the herb stalks out of the ruddy broth and add the reserved shellfish juices. Bring the broth to a gentle simmer, add the red mullet and cook it for about 3 minutes, then carefully scoop the fish out and keep it warm. Add the prawns to the broth and cook them for 2–3 minutes, or until they have turned pink. Stir in the basil and parsley, then add the mussels and clams, but not the red mullet.

When everything is hot divide the stew among 4 deep bowls, then carefully add the red mullet. Serve immediately, with a pile of paper napkins and debris bowls on the table.

more splodge some garlicky mayonnaise or rouille on top of each helping of stew. Chunks of sturdy bread would also be good.
less the stew is so flavoursome, you won't need anything else.

Seared scallops + black tagliolini

It's not absolutely imperative that you use black squid ink pasta for this dish, but it looks fabulously dramatic and adds an extra jot of flavour (and is available, currently, from Sainsbury's Special Selection). Otherwise, use any long, slender pasta, e.g. linguine or spaghettini. You will notice that I've suggested removing the coral from the scallops. This is the roe and it's perfectly edible. Personally, I am not wild about the texture and prefer to pound the coral into a butter (to glaze other fish), but don't let me sway you.

ingredients for 4

about 450g black squid ink tagliolini

70g pancetti cubetti (cubed pancetta)

4 garlic cloves
crushed and roughly chopped

4 large tomatoes
blanched, cored, de-seeded and roughly chopped

1 tbsp olive oil, plus a little extra

a very large handful of parsley
leaves roughly chopped

a few sprigs of fresh tarragon
leaves roughly chopped

12–20 large scallops (depending on size)
trimmed and corals removed

Cook the pasta in plenty of salted boiling water until just tender to the bite. Drain (reserving the water and keeping it at a simmer), run the pasta under cold water to stop the cooking, and then set aside.

Strew the pancetti cubetti into a large non-stick frying pan and place it over a medium flame. Cook the cubes until they are lightly gilded, tossing occasionally, then remove them and set aside. Add the garlic and cook for 2 minutes, stirring occasionally, then stir in the tomatoes and 1 tablespoon of olive oil. Cook for 2–3 minutes, then add the herbs and seasoning, and cook for a further 1–2 minutes. Pull the pan half off the heat so the sauce remains at a very idle simmer.

Using your hands, lightly oil the scallops, then season them. Heat a large heavy frying pan over a medium-high flame for 2 minutes, then arrange the scallops in it. Reduce the heat a little and cook them for 2 minutes, undisturbed. Turn the scallops and cook them for another 1–2 minutes or until the outsides are crusty-looking and the flesh is firm but still tender and juicy. Remove the pan from the heat.

Plunge the pasta back into the simmering cooking water, then pull the pan off the heat. Drain the pasta again and divide it among 4 serving plates. Spoon the sauce alongside the pasta, then perch the scallops on top. Finish with a scattering of the pancetta cubes (and the corals, if you are including them).

Baked hake + wheatgrain and roast vegetable hash

One rarely sees hake in this country – partly because of over-fishing but mostly because the Iberians nab it all. Cod, haddock and John Dory would all make fine substitutes. Fortunately wheatgrain (sometimes sold as 'pastawheat') is not under threat of extinction. It is rather like pearl barley, with a similar chewy, slippery texture. Everything needs cooking more or less simultaneously, with the veg kicking off first, and 10–15 minutes later the hake and wheatgrain. Make sure your frying pan has an ovenproof handle – most have.

ingredients for 4

3 medium courgettes
quartered lengthways and cut into small dice

250g cherry tomatoes

1 large mild chilli
de-seeded and thinly sliced

2 pinches of ground coriander

1 big pinch of fennel seeds

2 fresh or dried bay leaves
roughly torn

2 tsp olive oil, plus a little extra

2 tsp Marigold Swiss vegetable bouillon powder

200g wheatgrain

4 (about 175g) hake fillets, skin still on

a little plain flour

a large handful of parsley
leaves roughly chopped

a handful of fresh basil
leaves roughly torn

(to serve) 8 lemon wedges

Preheat the oven to 180°C fan/gas mark 6. Tumble the courgettes, tomatoes and chilli into a large roasting tin. Sprinkle with the coriander, fennel seeds and seasoning, then tuck in the bay leaves. Brush the vegetables with oil, then bake them for about 20–25 minutes, or until toasty looking and tender.

Meanwhile, half-fill a large saucepan with water, add the stock powder and bring to a boil, covered. Tip in the wheatgrain and cook it for about 15 minutes, or until tender, then drain and keep warm.

Lightly oil the fish and then dust it with seasoned flour. Heat a non-stick frying pan over a medium-high flame, put in the fish, skin-side down, and cook undisturbed for 3 minutes. Turn and cook for 1 minute. Transfer the pan to the oven for 6–10 minutes, until the fish is cooked.

Toss the wheatgrain and herbs with the veg. Check the seasoning, then spoon the hash on to 4 serving plates. Remembering the pan handle is hot, put the fish on top, crisp skin-side up. Serve with lemon.

more swish some extra olive oil over the fish.

Seared cod with green olive crust

'Family' magazines contain shoals of recipes for baked fish covered in indistinguishable carbohydrate-crumbed crusts. On the whole they share two characteristics – banality and a Gobi-like dryness. In contrast, this simple, sapid, moist crust reeks of sophistication. Well, I would say that, wouldn't I? The only naff factor is that mi-cuit tomatoes are now more commonly known as 'sunblush', a whimsical description devised by the supermarkets in their relentless and patronising commitment to obscuring the real provenance of foodstuffs.

ingredients for 4

8 tbsp green olive tapenade

6 mi-cuit tomatoes
chopped

a small handful of black olives
stoned and roughly chopped

1 garlic clove
crushed and finely chopped

a handful of flat leaf parsley
leaves chopped

a handful of fresh basil
leaves chopped

4 (about 175g) skinless cod fillets

a little olive oil

a little plain flour

Mix the tapenade, tomatoes, olives, garlic and herbs together and season with black pepper but not salt. Set the mixture aside for a moment. Very lightly oil the cod, using your hands, then dust it equally lightly with seasoned flour. Spread the tapenade mixture evenly over one side of each fillet.

Preheat the oven to 210°C fan/gas mark 8. Heat a large non-stick frying pan for a minute or two over a medium-high flame. Carefully put in the cod fillets, crust-side upwards, and cook them for 3–4 minutes. Checking first that the handle is heatproof – which it normally is – transfer the pan to the oven. Continue to cook the cod for another 6–10 minutes, or until the flesh is just opaque and the crust is toasty-brown.

more this needs nothing more complicated with it than a few new potatoes and some leafy spinach.
less leafy spinach is wonderful – have lots.

Rare beef salad + lime and chilli dressing

In this marvellous south-east Asian salad, the garlic, chilli, lime juice and fish sauce provide a searingly bright flavour, while the crushed peanuts add a sweet-savoury crunch, and the herbs just jangle with vibrancy. As usual, the making is far less painful than the length of the ingredients list suggests.

ingredients for 4

4 tbsp Thai fish sauce (nam pla)

1 tbsp dark soy sauce

3 tbsp groundnut oil, plus extra

a (600g) piece of well-hung beef fillet
trimmed scrupulously

1 small garlic clove
finely chopped

a dash of hot chilli sauce

1–2 tsp caster sugar

1–2 tbsp fresh lime juice

FOR THE SALAD

½ Chinese cabbage
halved, cored and sliced into thin ribbons

½ red pepper
de-seeded and sliced very finely

150g fresh beansprouts

a very large handful of fresh coriander
leaves picked off but left whole

3 bushy sprigs of fresh mint
leaves bundled up and finely sliced

a small handful of roast peanuts
roughly chopped

Combine half the fish sauce, all the soy sauce and 2 tablespoons of oil. Put the beef fillet in a close-fitting, non-reactive dish, then pour on the liquid and leave to marinate for 1 to 4 hours, turning the beef occasionally.

To make the dressing, whisk together the remaining fish sauce and oil, the garlic and chilli sauce, then add the smaller amount of sugar and lime juice. Add more sugar or lime to taste. Refrigerate for up to 48 hours.

To make the salad, pile all the ingredients, except the peanuts, into a large bowl and toss them together.

Preheat the oven to 200°C fan/gas mark 7. Remove the fillet, pat it dry with kitchen paper, then smear with a few drops of oil. Heat a heavy frying pan over a high flame. When it's smoking, quickly brown the beef on all sides. Transfer the frying pan to the oven and roast the beef for 10 minutes, then remove it (being careful to hold the handle with an oven cloth) and leave the fillet to cool before chilling it thoroughly in the fridge.

Slice the beef into narrow strips and toss them in half the dressing, using the rest for the salad. Divide the salad among 4 plates, pile the beef on top and finish with a scattering of peanuts – except for the dieter's plate.

One-pan Chinese chicken

Ken Hom obviously does it for millions of people, but so far I have managed to resist his allure: Ken Lo was my hero (until, on one occasion, I was placed next to him at dinner. Quite reasonably, extreme age and boredom with inconsequential dinner party chat rendered him rather less forthcoming than I had hoped). I dragged this recipe from a promotional booklet for a range of cast aluminium cookware for which the extant Ken has contributed recipes. Supposedly exclusive, it is as unremarkable and totally recognisable as any Chinese-style recipe you've ever seen, but anything which combines hoisin, chilli and soy sauce will always taste good.

ingredients for 4

600g boneless, skinless chicken thighs

I level tbsp cornflour

I tbsp toasted sesame oil

2 tbsp soy sauce

I tbsp groundnut (or vegetable) oil

3 garlic cloves
crushed and finely chopped

I tbsp chilli sauce

I tbsp hoisin sauce

I tbsp oyster sauce

I tsp caster sugar

a large handful of fresh basil
leaves bundled up and finely sliced

Cut the chicken into bite-sized chunks and put it in a non-reactive dish. Toss with the cornflour, sesame oil and I tablespoon of soy sauce, then set aside for 30 minutes.

Heat a very large wok over a medium-high flame, then add the groundnut oil. Swish it around and, when it's hot, put in the chicken. Stir-fry it for 3–4 minutes, or until just-cooked, then scoop out the chicken and discard the oil. Put back the chicken and add all the other ingredients, including the remaining soy sauce, but not the basil.

Cook for a further 5 minutes, tossing and/or stirring frequently, then add the basil and serve immediately.

more serve with bowls of steamed fragrant rice.
less spoon the chicken over fairly robust salad leaves, such as watercress, Little Gem, Chinese cabbage, red mustard or wild rocket, tossed with some fine strips of carrot, celery, red onion and/or cucumber.

Braised loin of pork + oregano and fennel

In this recipe, the pork is studded with garlic, then marinated before being lovingly braised with aromatic fennel and red wine. Use a traditional breed, such as Gloucester Old Spot, if you can, and ask the butcher to remove the skin from the pork and free, but not completely separate, the back bone from the meat.

ingredients for 4+

about 2kg free-range pork loin

4–6 garlic cloves
cut into fine slivers

3 tbsp olive oil

the juice of half a lemon

**4 bushy sprigs of fresh oregano
or thyme**
leaves only

about 250g shallots

a scrap of unsalted butter

2 fennel bulbs
outer leaves discarded, the rest cut into large chunks, with any feathery bits added to the marinade

about 400ml full-bodied red wine

Stab incisions all over the loin and insert a sliver of garlic into each hole. Put 2 tablespoons of the oil, the lemon juice and oregano in a large non-reactive dish, season with pepper and swish into a sludge. Massage the marinade into the pork and leave for 4 to 8 hours.

Cover the shallots with boiling water, leave them for 2 minutes, then rinse them under cold water and peel. Heat the remaining oil and butter in a large frying pan over a medium-high flame. Add the shallots and fennel, and fry for 6–8 minutes, stirring frequently, until pleasantly frazzled. Transfer the vegetables to a large cast-iron casserole. Reserve the frying pan.

Preheat the oven to 150°C fan/gas mark 3½. Scrape off the marinade and season the pork. Reheat the frying pan over a medium-high flame, quickly brown the joint on all sides, then put it in the casserole. Discard any fat in the pan, raise the heat, pour in the wine and boil rapidly for 2–3 minutes. Add all the nubbly liquid to the pork, transfer the casserole to the heat and bring the liquid to a boil. Put the casserole in the oven and cook for 90 minutes, turning the loin halfway through. Leave to rest, still covered, for about 15 minutes before serving.

more the pork cries out for potatoes, roast or mashed.

PUDDINGS

Sparkling muscat (or other fruit) jelly

In this beautiful dessert, aromatic muscat grapes dance in sparkling Italian Prosecco jelly. If it's not the right season for muscat grapes (as was the case when we did the photography for this book), use raspberries or blueberries instead. Winter grapes from the southern hemisphere are tough, tasteless and not worth a pip.

ingredients for 6

300ml hot water

55g caster sugar

**500ml Prosecco
(or any dryish sparkling wine)**

4 gelatine leaves

150g muscat grapes
halved and de-seeded

Put the water and sugar into a small saucepan over a low-medium flame. Stir to dissolve the crystals, then raise the heat and bring to a boil. Reduce the heat, simmer for 5 minutes, then remove the pan.

Meanwhile, pour the Prosecco into a large heatproof bowl and add the gelatine. Set aside for about 5 minutes, or until the leaves are soft and squidgy. Take out the leaves, squeeze off as much liquid as possible, and add them to the sugar syrup. Whisk furiously until the gelatine has completely dissolved, then pour the syrup back into the bowl with the Prosecco and whisk to combine.

Allow to cool thoroughly, then refrigerate the jelly for about 1 hour. As soon as it starts to thicken, stir in the grapes. Divide the jelly among 6 beautiful glasses, cover them with clingfilm, and refrigerate for 4 to 6 hours, or until they have completely set.

Rosy fruit terrine

Yes folks, it's yet another jelly, albeit in a very adult disguise. Although I've specified particular berries, feel free to change them as your palate and the season dictate. Don't use blackcurrants, though, or any fruit that requires a preliminary cooking.

ingredients for 6+

600ml rosé wine

5 gelatine leaves

115g refined caster sugar

450g Alpine or wild strawberries (or blueberries)

115g raspberries

115g white currants
stripped from their stalks

FOR THE FLAVOURED CREAM

1 (284ml) carton whipping cream

2 tbsp caster sugar

2–3 tbsp cassis (or framboise, mûre or cerise) liqueur

Pour half the rosé into a large heatproof bowl and add the gelatine. Leave for 5 minutes, or until the gelatine is soft and squidgy.

Put the rest of the rosé, 100ml cold water and the sugar into a small heavy pan over a low flame and stir until the crystals have dissolved. Raise the heat and bring to a boil, then simmer for 5 minutes. Remove the pan from the heat and pour the syrup into the bowl with the rosé and gelatine. Whisk furiously until the leaves have completely dissolved.

Mix the fruits together, then arrange some of them in a single layer in the bottom of a 1kg loaf tin (reserving the rest). Pour in just enough jelly to 'fix' them in place – don't submerge them or they will float. Refrigerate the jelly for about 30 minutes or until it has set, but keep the remaining jelly warm enough to pour. Arrange another layer of fruit in the tin and pour over enough jelly to barely cover. Refrigerate until set. Repeat until the berries and the jelly are both used up. Refrigerate for 6–8 hours, or until completely set.

Whisk the cream and sugar into soft peaks, then whisk in the fruit liqueur to taste. Dip the outside of the terrine into very hot water for 10–15 seconds, then invert the jelly on to a flat serving dish. Cut the terrine into thick slices and serve.

more have a dollop of sensuous cream with the jelly.
less nix.

Mango and lime granita

Unlike sorbet, Italian *granita* (*granite* in French) is a soft mass of jagged crystals, rather like a stiffish 'slush puppy'. It's best made only a few hours before being served: if you make it much earlier, then you may have to defrost it slightly and fork up the crystals to get the right consistency. (You can also 'pulse' them in a food processor, but you will lose some of the essential crystalline coarseness.) Do make sure the fruit is really ripe (including the limes, which are better bought when yellow-flushed, rather than deepest green).

ingredients for 4+

600ml hot water

350g granulated sugar

1 large ripe mango

the juice of 3 juicy limes

a little lemon juice

(to serve) lime wedges

Combine the water and sugar in a heavy saucepan over a low-medium heat. Stir until the crystals have dissolved, then raise the heat and bring to a boil. Remove the pan and leave the syrup to cool completely.

Meanwhile, cut down either side of the mango stone to remove the 2 'cheeks'. Using a small sharp knife, pare away the skin from the narrow pelmet of flesh that surrounds the stone, then slice off all the flesh. Everything is going into a blender, so it would be good if you could do this over the open jug to capture all the juices. Now criss-cross the flesh of each 'cheek', cutting down right to the skin. Push up from the skin side so the mango inverts and the flesh pops up like a chunky orange hedgehog. Slice off the cubes and put them in the blender, then repeat with the other half. Add the lime juice and whizz the fruit to a smooth purée.

Push the purée through a fine sieve into the syrup. Whisk thoroughly to combine, then taste and add enough lemon juice to bring out the flavours. Pour the fruit syrup into a plastic container and freeze for 1–2 hours, or until ice crystals start to form around the edge. Using a fork, mash the frozen part back into the liquid, then continue freezing. Fork up the crystals every hour or so, until you they have formed a crystalline mass. Serve the *granita* in small wine glasses or tumblers, with a wedge of lime.

Nice easy (cooked) things to do with fresh fruit

The idea of cooking fruit shouldn't be thought of as merely a wintry thing – in fact the fruits which take to being cooked best of all are rhubarb and gooseberries, which appear in late spring and early summer respectively. (It's surprising, too, how many fruits that we normally eat raw take kindly to a little sojourn in the heat.) Unfortunately, the best cooked-fruit dishes are not compatible with a slimming diet: crumbles, cobblers, tarts and pies are all laden under the weight of sugar, butter and flour. Nevertheless, the sketchy recipes below should give you some idea on how to lift the mundane into the slightly spectacular – although nothing could ever be as good as gooseberry crumble with Jersey cream.

Bananas can be: baked or grilled whole, the flesh then sprinkled with dark rum, a pinch of powdered ginger and lime juice, then strewn with lime zest; baked or grilled whole, the flesh spooned out and eaten with a dusting of ground cinnamon or cocoa powder and a spoonful of Greek low-fat yoghurt.

Cherries can be: stoned and simmered in redcurrant jelly, a dash of water, drop of kirsch and a pinch of cinnamon – and eaten warm, or cooled and folded into low-fat Greek yoghurt.

Figs can be: halved or cut criss-cross style and opened up, then dotted with crumbled goat's cheese and grilled; sprinkled with rosewater and a dab of honey and grilled; dolloped with spoonfuls of low-fat Greek yoghurt and a dab of honey, and grilled.

Peaches can be: cut in half, stoned, sprinkled with Marsala and a few drops of vanilla extract, and grilled or baked; stuffed with crushed amaretti and a dash of amaretto, grilled, and served with raspberry sauce.

Pineapple can be: cut into thin slices, sprinkled with dark rum, kirsch or gin, grilled and strewn with a crumbled amaretti biscuit; cut into slices, grilled and drizzled with passion fruit juice or orange juice.

Rhubarb can be: dusted with sugar and ground star anise and baked in a single layer for 8 minutes at high temperature; sprinkled with ground cinnamon (or ginger) and grated orange zest, baked, mixed with a crushed amaretti biscuit and eaten immediately (while the biscuit remains crunchy); baked and sprinkled with rosewater and a few drops of vanilla (try it without sugar first); dusted with ground cardamom, baked and folded into low-fat Greek yoghurt for a dietary fool.

Winter fruit salad

A small compensation for our dreary winter is that tropical fruits are at their best. I love a proper, carefully made English fruit salad, but an exotic fruit salad can provide different though just as pleasing flavours. (I use the word 'exotic' inadvisedly: these fruits are now commonplace, but we still need some way of differentiating them from northern-hemisphere fruits.)

It's pointless giving exact quantities because everything depends on what is available and, more importantly, what's in good nick – a mango that's as hard as a pumpkin (and likely to stay that way for a few days) is no good to anyone. I'd also avoid star fruit (because they look pretty but taste of crisp water), persimmon (because they never seem to ripen), kiwi fruit (because they look naff even though they are not as flavourless as some would have you believe, especially when ripe) and any fruit from South Africa, Israel or Kenya – not for political reasons but because most of it is so stupidly tasteless. Finally, make sure there's a good balance between sweetness and acidity, and plenty of juice to bathe the fruits in.

ingredients for 6

about 1kg exotic fruit chosen from:
pineapple, mango, pawpaw, guava, lychee, passionfruit, tangerine, coconut (shaved), orange, custard apple, pomegranate and fresh dates

1 tbsp rosewater

1–2 tbsp lemon juice

Peel and prepare the fruit according to its individual characteristics, remembering to catch all the juices over a bowl. If you are cutting the fruit into cubes, don't make them too small: the salad will look unstylish and the texture will verge on the mushy.

Gently toss the fruit with all the reserved juices, adding rosewater and lemon juice, to taste. If you need to add any sugar (you shouldn't), then use icing sugar so it dissolves properly. As long as you don't use any bananas (or, at least, not until the last minute), the fruit salad will keep for 24 hours, clingfilmed and refrigerated.

Spiced fruit compote

It took me a long time to recover from the dread of dried fruit incurred by countless ghastly school dinners. A starving orphan would have been able to resist those awful saggy prunes swilling around in nameless fluid, with lumpy custard dumped on top. Nowadays I appreciate how good a fruit compote can be when the poaching liquid purrs with zippy flavours and the fruits retain some textural contrast. Play around with different combinations – weak Earl Grey tea jazzed up with root ginger is another good poaching broth. If you can, segment the oranges over the syrup to catch as much juice as possible: squeeze the juice out of the debris too.

ingredients for 6+

1 (75cl) bottle of light fruity red wine

150g natural caster sugar

2 vanilla pods
split lengthways

1 fresh or dried bay leaf

1 cinnamon stick

12–16 whole black peppercorns

250g unsulphured dried apricots

400g Agen prunes (or mi-cuit plums)

3 large oranges
peel and pith removed, then
cut into skinless segments

Put all the ingredients, except the fruits, into a large saucepan over a medium flame. Bring the liquid to a boil, uncovered. Rapidly boil for 5 minutes, then add any juice from the oranges. Put in the apricots and prunes (but not the oranges) and return to a boil. Immediately reduce the heat and gently simmer the fruits for 10 minutes. Pull the pan aside, gently stir in the orange segments and leave to cool. Chill the compote for at least 2 hours before serving: it will keep for several days, refrigerated.

more serve the compote with toasted slices of *pain d'épice*, the honey-spiced cake that's normally sold in cellophane-wrapped 'bricks.' Crème fraîche or a dab of mascarpone would be nice, too.
less stick with the compote.

French apple tarts

Isn't apple tart the best? While it's not the most obviously frugal of puddings, surprisingly there are less than 300 calories to each of these tarts, if you forgo the crème fraîche. Serve them after a light main course, such as crab salad, and don't fret. If you can find all-butter puff pastry, collar a packet immediately: it's much better flavoured than the normal stuff.

ingredients for 6

2–3 tbsp Calvados

250g crème fraîche

1 (about 350g) pkt of ready-rolled puff pastry

3 fairly acidic dessert apples (e.g. new season Cox's, Braeburn)
peeled, cored and very thinly sliced

30g unsalted butter
melted

30–55g light muscovado sugar

Stir 2–3 tablespoons of Calvados into the crème fraîche to taste, and set aside in a cool place.

Preheat the oven to 220°C fan/gas mark 8. Roll out the shorter side of the pastry by a couple of inches, until the sheet is squarer-looking. Cut the pastry into six evenly sized pieces, trimming off any raggedy edges with a sharp knife. (Don't compress the edges or the pastry will not rise.) Arrange the pastries on a heavy non-stick baking sheet. With the point of a knife, mark a 'frame' a scant half-centimetre in from the edge of each piece. (This will result in a raised border.)

Starting at a short side, lay 2 rows of overlapping apple slices side-by-side down each piece of pastry, tight to the border. Brush the apples with melted butter, then strew with sugar to taste. Cook the tarts on a middle shelf of the oven for about 15 minutes, or until the pastry is golden and puffy, and the apples have wilted.

Serve while still warm but not burning hot.

more have a big splodge of the Calvados crème fraîche.
less be thankful for what you have.

the CATCH 22 of EXERCISING

"Every thin woman wants to grow plump", wrote Brillat-Savarin, the French politician and gourmet. Well, they may have done in 1825, when his eternally fascinating book, *The Physiology of Taste*, was published. Nowadays I think most women subscribe to the 'you can never be too rich or too thin' philosophy. Brillat-Savarin's advice about how to put on weight is actually very funny, sometimes intentionally, sometimes because nineteenth-century nutritional science was a bit sketchy. But when it comes to his thoughts about exercise, I am with Brillat-Savarin all the way when he says, "If you do not take any exercise, you will be inclined to grow fat; if you exercise, you will still grow fat, since you will eat more than usual." Tell me about it. Never will I forget the day I cycled 25 miles, having eaten fairly immoderately the day before, but with only a modest lunch on the day of the bike ride, and found the next day that I had gained two pounds. Outrageous.

But I am jumping the gun, because I didn't even get on a bike until I had lost over three stone, and there's the rub (as my poor crotch can vouchsafe). The unassailable, irrefutable fact is that if you really are fat it doesn't matter how much your heart and brain command you to exercise, your body simply cannot obey the instruction. This does not apply to those people just a few pounds overweight: I am talking about real fatties, like me. The blubber that billowed round my body, like puppies playing on a beanbag, would not allow me to do anything more than waddle around. It was just too damned difficult. For a start, I couldn't bend properly because my breasts, belly and thighs merged into one huge, inflexible bolster. I couldn't even raise one leg because I didn't have any muscles capable of lifting the weight. Worst of all, it was impossible to breathe: static exercise was bad enough, but any faintly vigorous movement induced more gasping and panting than you'd find in a soft-porn film.

The pressure to exercise comes from all quarters. Doctors' surgeries are papered like Beijing's Democracy Wall with urgent entreaties to stop smoking, have regular smear tests – and take exercise. Magazines and newspapers never stop banging on about it. How many times have you read that you should take the stairs, not the lift; get off the bus or train one stop before your destination and walk the rest of the way; or exercise briskly enough to raise your heartbeat for at least three 30-minute periods each week? At the health clinic, I felt guilty if I didn't tip up to the underwater exercise class (which, funnily enough, I might have done if it hadn't been at such an ungodly hour) or the general exercise class or the Pilates class. Of course, those who did were, unsurprisingly, the least fat.

Stuff it all, say I. Whom do all these well-meaning authorities think they are targeting? Slim fit people are that way either because they don't eat much or because they are blessed with slim fit genes or because they exercise like hell and enjoy it. Fat people are that way either because they eat too much or are damned with fat genes or because they don't exercise and hate the very thought of it. You may as well ask a vulture to ignore a dead carcass as entreat a really fat person to exercise. It's a waste of time – and it's unnecessary. I can say that with impunity, partly because this book is not about political correctness, as I've already made clear, but mostly because I myself have lost a large amount of weight without doing a scrap of formal exercise.

While I don't entirely subscribe to his overall dieting philosophy, I was interested to see that Michel Montignac, the author of *Dine Out and Lose Weight*, espouses the same philosophy. Famous for his high-fat, low-carb diet, Monsieur Montignac also believes that "Exercise has never caused anyone to lose weight". He goes on to say, "When you exercise you are spending energy from your temporary reserves (glycogen) which are fuelled by your consumption of carbohydrates. The first time you get back into exercising you may indeed notice about a four ounce difference in your weight. If you exercise regularly, your body will align its 'supply' with your new demands. If your demands increase, your body will quickly start stocking enough glycogen to satisfy your energy requirements. You will very soon notice that not only are you not losing pounds but may be back at your initial weight. You may even have gained a little. If your physical exertion increases, your body will not only produce more energy, it will stock up its fat reserves. And so the vicious circle begins."

Sadly, I believe this to be true, viz. my cycle ride. However, he does admit – and I think it's very important – that exercising can be good for your soul. I may not have exercised in order to lose weight but during my stay at Shrublands last year (after the big weight loss), I decided I would give the Pilates class a proper whirl. For six days I stretched and breathed, breathed and stretched. To my surprise, and not a little worry, I found myself actively enjoying the sessions, to the point where I purchased a big rubber ball (for squeezing), a mat (to lie on), a pair of three-pound weights (for arm whirling), and a tape (to remind myself of what to do).

Eight months down the line (including the Christmas period – a test if ever there was one), I find myself doing Pilates for an hour, if not every day, then at least three times a week. Frankly, I'm amazed: after 30-odd years of sneering I've joined the ranks of those who enjoy exercise.

What you should never do, even if you do think you've been ensnared by the exercising bug, is rush out and join an expensive gym. It's common knowledge that only a tiny percentage of the membership ever exploits the facilities to a level that justifies the fee. (Don't forget there's always a 'joining' fee, that you will never get back. If you use the gym frequently this fee is effectively amortised over the first year but, if you don't, it makes the financial loss substantially greater.) What normally happens is that after the first thrill of rushing to the gym (in new leotard or track suit) there follows a feeling of inertia and mild dread at the very thought of exercising. It's always too cold, too hot, too late, too early, too disruptive – too anything you care to invent as an excuse. The only beneficiary of your optimistic plan to exercise regularly is the company that owns the gym, as they happily bank your monthly (by direct debit, naturally) non-returnable, unused subscription. No, if you find yourself in the grip of an urge to work out communally, join a local council gym. You may not find yourself in the social circle to which you aspire, nor will there be slate and wengé interiors, but the equipment will be as good as any private gym and there will be just as much of it. The best part is that there won't be a joining fee, nor will you have to take out an entire year's subscription.

Of course, formal exercise may never be your thing. Gym sessions take place indoors for a start, whereas walking gives you the opportunity to revel in the scenery, observe the odd bit of wildlife, feel the wind biting your ears or the sunshine warming your face.

Personally, I have recently rediscovered my youthful love of cycling (despite the 25 mile/2lb weight gain). There's something about the height at which one sits (encouraging a good view over the hedgerows); the moderate speed (fast enough to prevent boredom but slow enough to allow a good gawp); the silence (that means you can sneak up on birds or animals and catch them unawares); and the general manoeuvrability of a bike (allowing off-track sorties and parking right next to the pub wall - shhhurely not). If the idea of cycling leaves you as cold as a supermarket sandwich it's still worth finding something slightly energetic to do. (Apparently, romping round the bedroom counts.) If all else fails, just move a bit more quickly. I am not kidding. You'd be amazed at how few calories you use sitting slumped at a desk all day or driving a car. Even pushing the lawn mower, painting the living room or going to a football match – anything that requires a little action – will increase the calories you burn.

I have one final idea: volunteer your services as a part-time waitress (or waiter) at your local restaurant. I am being absolutely serious. All restaurants are crying out for staff, especially part-timers who will augment the permanent team at weekends, during busy holiday periods or at outside catering events. Okay, they may not offer you a job at Gordon Ramsay, and I am not suggesting you should stand behind the counter in a hamburger joint with a humiliating lack of stars pinned to your uniform jacket – but there are thousands of small owner-run restaurants and hotels that would love to employ someone bright and cheerful for a few hours a week. The advantage is that you will walk further in one evening than if you were doing the Paris to Dakar race (well, that's for cars, but you know what I mean). In between nursing your aching feet, you will also have a lot of fun. Being behind the scenes in a restaurant is a real eye-opener, as you find out just how horrible, strange, exacting or nice customers can be. Another obvious advantage is that you will also earn some money.

But the main reason you will lose weight is not so much to do with the miles you tramp as the fact that you won't have any time to eat. It's quite amazing: you will see more wonderful food in a few hours than you've had in a month, but it belongs to the customer – although if you're very lucky you may be able to grab the odd chip from a bowl coming back to the wash-up. Never do I eat so little as when I am working at the Crown and Castle.

If you are beginning to feel there is a mass of contradiction associated with exercising, you'd be right. But the main points are these: first, you do not need to exercise to lose weight; second, don't expect weight loss automatically to accompany exercise; third, the easiest way to exercise is simply to increase your normal daily activity level; fourth, the benefits of exercise are more to do with your soul than your hips; and, finally, working in a restaurant is the answer. And that's my last word on the subject.

HELP!

Monday, 3rd February 2003 – I am not so much struggling as desperate. I've just weighed myself and the horrible truth is that in the last five months I have gradually – very gradually, compared to my pre-diet days – gained eight pounds. I've always talked about having lost four stone and that's true. In fact, at one point I'd actually lost over four stone – but that was after a week in Shrublands, closely followed by a bout of gastroenteritis, so I didn't get over-excited.

But I can't pretend – I have got fatter and, worse still, I've also lost control. The evidence is apparent in my car: an empty sandwich carton and a Magnum wrapper. My excuse is that I was trapped in the usual horrendous Friday night rear-light trail getting out of London and, knowing that the journey would take at least three hours, I thought I'd have a quick snack. I virtuously chose a free-range egg salad sandwich with no mayonnaise and a sub-250 calorie content, but then scuppered the whole lark by buying an ice cream. The inexcusable part is that the petrol station's freezer was well stocked with modestly caloried milk lollies but, instead, I went for a stonking great Magnum. If this were a one-off incident it wouldn't matter, but it isn't. I've gradually started buying bags of toffees, boiled sweets and/or mints, swearing that I will only suck one or two, but have then scoffed the lot in two sessions. Bread has not so much slunk back into my diet as stormed in like a wheat-charged tornado. After the sandwich and ice cream debacle, I found myself nicking not one slice of bread but two from my husband's late-night post-work snack – not to mention a wedge of Camembert to go with it. (I may as well go the whole hog and tell you that I also ate an apple, two-thirds of a Geo bar – I selflessly let the dogs have the remainder – and, oh hang my head in shame, shame and more shame – a bag of flying saucers.)

It also hasn't helped that I've just got back from Paris where, needless to say, I went wild. Wading into vast *assiettes* of shellfish was not too bad, but I can't excuse eating every bit of bread that came my way or drinking every glass of wine that was poured. I justified my vast intake by the endless walking we did, but any hope that I might have balanced out the energy intake against the energy expenditure was completely undone by my activities on the last day, when I bought eight different cheeses to bring home. (Yes, of course I ate them, with some help, I hasten to add.) The interesting thing is that in the past, when slim friends have bemoaned a weight gain of this magnitude, I have been overtly scornful. After all, what's a piddly half-stone to someone who is walking around looking like a roll of roof insulation. It's only now that I realise why they became so distressed: putting on weight is not so much to do with tight waistbands as the feeling of being as powerless as a wind-blown paper bag.

But there is a positive side to my current crisis: I may be desperate but I am not in a blind panic, nor am I letting the situation get any worse. This is because I've learned one of the keys to this dieting business and that is to accept that it's impossible to alter one's innate character – hone it, temper it, mould it, ameliorate it, maybe, but that's as far as it goes. Changing one's lifestyle is possible, at a stretch, but not one's essential being. So, if you love eating you will inevitably experience the odd fall from grace when circumstances become difficult. Like any other addiction, you may be in remission but you will never be cured.

The first rule is – don't panic when things go wrong

Realising that it's not me that has to change but what I do, means that I also know I can start again. Previously I have always adopted the 'hung for a sheep' philosophy. You know – the one where because you've had a bacon sandwich you go on to eat an entire box of Smarties. Then, because the scales have gone up the next day, you have two helpings of lasagne, as well as a slice of carrot cake and a milk-shake. At this point you think all is lost. Well, it isn't. Miraculously, God gives us another day. And it doesn't have to be a Monday or New Year's Day, it can be any day, even the current one. So stop right now. A few pounds is not so very difficult to lose, but let it mount up and suddenly it's not Primrose Hill you have to scale but Kilimanjaro. Anyway, the great thing about having a blow-out, when you've been dieting for an extended period, is that getting back on track can be quite thrilling. The reason? Because you can clearly remember the physical benefits from when you were eating (and drinking) healthily. Reacquiring that feeling of lightness and clarity, as well as an absence of aches and pains, means that saying 'goodbye' to stodge and 'hello' to sprightly food can be a positive pleasure. For myself, I am now dieting again but with only eight pounds to lose, not four stone.

The second rule is – you can always start again

Being back on track doesn't mean the cravings will suddenly disappear. One of the most futile sentences I hear myself uttering is, 'Please don't let me eat any bread.' (Substitute your own nemesis food.) All this does is breed tremendous resentment when the appellee tries to prevent the perpetrator from tucking into a thick slab of sourdough toast spread with loganberry jam. And, as soon as the coast is clear, you'll do the dastardly deed anyway. No, it's a disagreeable fact that only you can be the guardian of your diet – and conscience. The good part is that once the right mind-set has been attained you can eat with impunity, however taxing the circumstances.

One of the best ways of ensuring this happy state is to build in, quite purposefully, an indulgence day. Plan it in advance so it's something to look forward to, and eat only your favourite food, be it chocolate, cheese, ice cream or chips. This has a double benefit. First, you'll be pleasantly surprised at how deeply unsatisfying many dream foods turn out to be. Not always, of course, but when it comes down to it, most commercial biscuits and cakes are full of sweet nothing. After a period of abstinence, the sheer artificiality of processed food is revealed in its true light – and there's nothing like resentment for turning marshmallow into saccharine shaving foam.

Second, you may well discover that at least half the thrill of eating so-called prohibited foods is simply because they are forbidden. Take away the guilt factor and they quickly lose their allure. You could even find yourself halfway through an indulgence day craving some cottage cheese and rice cakes. (Okay, that's pushing it a bit far, I agree.) The main thing is to luxuriate fully in your 'day off'. Wallow in it, have a fabulous time. Don't count the cost, because there won't be any. Tomorrow you'll be back in gear and by the end of the week any possible repercussions will have vanished from the scales. Remember, you like food and that's fine.

The third rule is – build in a dedicated indulgence day

Human nature being what it is, there are times when one is simply overpowered by the desire to eat something both rubbishy and highly calorific. While I am not advocating a complete loss of discipline each and every time this occurs, sometimes the temptation is too much. I once remember standing in our local health food shop and espying, amidst the usual array of peanut butter-linked products, a chocolate bar of super-appalling content. Reese's Nutrageous is as fat-ridden as it sounds (but being American, the packaging doesn't need to list any nutritional information, so I can't tell you exactly how much). I had to try it. The only way to deal with the problem was to swing my patent anti-gorging technique into action. So, the bar was purchased, the car was entered, the seat belt fastened and the engine started. The wrapper was removed and – vital, this part – I opened the window. I took a bite of the stupendously sickly chocolate with its sticky, chewing, nutty, peanut filling. I chewed, then swallowed it. A few seconds later I took a second bite and – simultaneously – chucked the rest out of the window. Not the wrapper, just the chocolate – it's important to uphold some standards. The deed was done. My craving was satisfied but my calorie intake was a fifth of what it would have been had I eaten the whole bar.

It's not only when tempted by obvious rubbish that this technique can be utilised. (Although it helps being in a car – remember Miranda in *Sex in the City*, retrieving the chocolate cake from the bin?) I do a similar thing with other foods. When I cut an avocado in half I don't eat the whole pear, but either carefully clingfilm one half for a later meal or give the extra to my husband. If I can't resist the tray of chunky oven-baked skin-on chips that are sitting on the hot-plate ready for staff supper, I take one, have a bite and immediately throw the rest away. I'm not saying I don't come back for a second chip, but at least it means I've only eaten a total of one at the end of the day, not two. Even when I open a tiny bag of low-fat pretzels, I immediately dump a third in the bin (or Jessie and Jack's mouths). You could call this pathetic, and you'd be right. I don't care – if it works I'll do it.

The fourth rule is – have a mouthful, then throw the rest away

Short car journeys may be tolerable but long-distance travelling presents the dieter with immense problems. Quite simply there is nowhere – and I do not exaggerate – where you can eat decent, reasonably slimming food when you are on the road. (The same is true of most trains, boats and planes, although the food on Danish ferries is something of an honourable exception.) It's not just the chain 'restaurants', such as MacDonalds or Little Chef, that are at fault: 99% of roadside pubs major on big, bulky carbohydrate-based food and/or deep-fried processed protein. You can't really blame them, because if there is one thing that characterises the average British diner it's an admiration for plates piled up like a landfill site. As for puddings, the stodgier, stickier, sweeter or creamier something is, the better. I doubt if there is another country, apart from the USA, where people are encouraged to eat themselves silly or where 'death by chocolate' is meant to be amusing, even though it's all too likely to occur.

Of course, some of these places do have salads on their menus, but I am not sure what tinned sweetcorn, gloopy coleslaw, vinegary beetroot, pappy tomatoes and a bit of iceberg lettuce have to do with the sprightly, fresh composition that normally connotes salad. Frankly, the chances of garnering a healthy lunch while on the move are remote.

So, knowing that I am going to be under pressure the moment I set foot in a vehicle I drop swiftly into Girl Guide mode. Into the car goes a bottle of Badoit, closely followed by a clutch of apples and bananas, a Geo bar and plenty of chewing gum. If it's only a two-hour trip to London, that will do. For longer trips, I try to plan the journey so we pass an M&S or Prêt à Manger on the way. With cold-bag suitably prepared, I stuff it with mayo-free sandwiches or sushi, smoothies, crudités, loads of fruit, roast chicken thighs, composed salads – or whatever else they have to offer. Travelling to Paris on Eurostar – where the food is ill-conceived and shamefully bad – I've even been known to take a mixing bowl with me, so that I could properly toss the Caesar salads I had purchased for our party. Even if you ignore the dieting aspect, the standard of food available to travellers is, on the whole, quite appalling. For years I have longed to have enough money to set up my own chain of roadside cafés, starting with the A12 and M11. It's not likely to happen, but if there's anyone out there with the dosh and the desire to offer drivers simple, decent food, may I please be your consultant.

The fifth rule is – take your own food when travelling

Travelling or not, dieters should always be thinking about where the next meal is coming from. The odd thing is that although I subscribe to this philosophy, I also find it anathema. Why should food, and the consumption of it, take up so much time and brainpower? Half of me says life's too short for this kind of nonsense; the other half of me knows that life will definitely be too short if I carry on eating willy-nilly. So, boring and painful though it is, I always try to make sure I am surrounded with the right kind of food, especially the right kind of snacks.

I was recently watching a television programme about how, within a year or so, even successful slimmers ended up fat again. They showed a succession of pea-brained, quadruple-chinned mammoths with huge, pendulous breasts (and that was just the men), and I got more and more depressed. Then they switched to a pleasant, up-beat woman of no great beauty or acumen, who had bucked the trend and managed to avoid regaining all the weight she had lost.

She proudly showed the camera her fridge and, no surprise to me, it was completely stuffed with low-calorie, readily accessible snacks. Okay, I didn't quite share her enthusiasm for cockles in vinegar, but the tubs of rollmops, cartons of low-fat yoghurt and cottage cheese, oodles of salading, and packets of prawns, smoked mackerel and gravlax, struck a real chord. She had not only learned how to lose weight, but more importantly how to keep it off. Particularly, she understood that it isn't meal times that present the greatest threat to slimmers, but the long hours in between. You alone will know when you are most likely to crumble under the pressure of wanting to eat. You will also know that these occasions rarely have anything to do with genuine hunger. But it's at these times that you must be able to march straight into the kitchen and grab something relatively innocuous – something that replenishes the coffers, without breaking the bank.

The sixth rule is – fill the house with healthy snacks

Whether this last bit appears in print will depend very much on whether my (really nice) publishers accept that this has to be an honest account of my diet, even though some parts of it may be unacceptable. Once in a while, when I overeat, I make myself sick. Yes, I know, this is dangerous, stupid and no one in their right mind should ever contemplate doing it. But – and it's a personal, unqualified 'but' – I know that I am neither anorectic, nor am I bulimic. What's more, I am never likely to be. I simply like good food too much. (Which means that I do not think a dry sultana scone that has been split open, filled with a squirt of aerosol cream and garnished with an out-of-season strawberry, is a treat. There is a universe of difference between a devastatingly good Little Red Barn chocolate brownie and a chocolate-flavoured muffin.)

Anyway, getting back to the thorny subject of (very) occasional self-induced vomiting, it has always been after a restaurant meal where I have thrown caution to the wind and eaten far too much food, and drunk far too much wine. It's important to stress that the ensuing action has had very little to do with food-associated guilt and everything to do with feeling physically uncomfortable. It's also important to stress that I do not advocate this as a slimming technique, especially if you are remotely frail mentally or have any history of eating disorders. What's perhaps even more noteworthy is that the next morning the scales have always gone up, not down! So, as a method of losing weight, it doesn't actually work.

The seventh rule is – if you overeat, it's stupid to make yourself sick

It will probably sound as if I am contradicting everything I've said so far if I now warn you not to be too serious about dieting. The fact is, I do think one has to treat the whole thing as something of a game, albeit an increasingly important one as you get older and fatter. I am aware that this may sound hypocritical, given that the whole thrust of this book is how to manage your food intake. But life goes on (and look how insouciant someone as talented, funny and pretty Dawn French is about her size). If you allow yourself to think of dieting as a straitjacket that won't be released until you weigh less than a ten-year-old, or are dead, you will drive yourself crazy. Of course, you will eat too much sometimes. And you will get depressed and wonder whether it's worth it. And you will hate having to rein yourself in, when all you really want to do is gallop off clutching a family-size pack of Maltesers. Well, fine – that's what happens in real life. Keep this whole dieting thing in proportion. It's not like having terminal cancer. Just get on with it, do the best you can – and always, always remember, tomorrow is another day.

The final (apparently contradictory) rule is – there's more to life than dieting

a few useful web-site addresses

www.clearspring.co. uk – oriental foods, including Mitoku concentrated shiitake broth

www.goodnessdirect.co.uk – distributor of Sanchi Japanese foods

www.savoria.co.uk – good Italian artisanal food supplier

www.martins-seafresh.co.uk – a very reliable shellfish and fish supplier

www.freshfood.co.uk – organic fruit and vegetable supplier

www.islandseafare.co.uk – smoked salmon and shellfish supplier

www.french-truffle.com – reasonably priced and reliable black truffle supplier

SOD IT

Hot bitter chocolate mousse + thick Jersey cream

If you're going to blow your diet, at least do it with some style and not on a packet of cheap crisps or a stupidly sweet creme egg. I can't think of a better way to go than with this fabulous essence-of-chocolate mousse – nor could our customers, who insist that it's always on the menu at the Crown and Castle. Quite simply, it's stunningly good. Be aware, you need to melt the chocolate, whisk the egg yolk mixture (in the mixer) and beat the egg whites more or less simultaneously.

ingredients for 6

200g bitter chocolate (about 70% cocoa solids)
roughly broken

100g unsalted butter, plus a scrap

6 large eggs
yolks and whites separated

100g caster sugar

30g cocoa powder, plus a little extra

(to serve) thick Jersey cream

Preheat the oven to 180°C fan/gas mark 6. Put the chocolate and 100g of butter into a small heavy saucepan and melt it very gently over the lowest, diffused flame. (Better still, use a microwave or bain-marie.)

Beat the egg yolks and sugar with electric beaters for a good 5 minutes, until the mixture has about doubled in volume and is soft and voluptuous, then whisk in the 30g of cocoa powder. Scrape the melted chocolate and butter into the mixture and whisk just long enough to combine.

Whisk the egg whites until they form soft peaks. They should not be quite as shiny and firm as for meringues but must definitely hold their shape.

Add a quarter of the egg whites to the chocolate mixture and whisk to combine. Now change to a large metal kitchen spoon and carefully fold in the remaining egg white. (The aim, at all times, is to keep as much air in the mixture as possible.)

Very lightly butter 6 ramekins (about 10cm diameter). Spoon in the mixture, leaving a scant 1cm clearance at the top. Put the ramekins on a heavy baking sheet and cook them for about 10 minutes on the middle shelf of the oven, or until they have risen. (It will be a gentle, not massive, rise.) Dust the tops very lightly with cocoa powder and serve immediately, together with a bowl of thick cream: you can spoon it in once the first mouthful has been removed. Eat, and enjoy every last scrap.

And, remember, all is not lost – you can begin dieting again at the very next meal!

index

recipe list with approximate calories per serving

Although I keep a rough tally of the calories I am consuming during the course of the day, it is only that – rough. Personally, I don't count veg or fruit at all (unless it's something very starchy, such as potatoes or bananas), nor do I regard good lean protein, such as chicken or fish, as being 'expensive' because the calories are used so efficiently. However, for those more exercised by these things than me, you will find below an approximate guide to how many calories are in the dieter's portion, next to the recipe title. The thing to remember is that the count is necessarily variable (especially in the recipes for a number of non-dieting people), because I can't monitor how much rice you eat, or how many drops of oil you use to anoint a piece of fish. So, don't dismiss a recipe just because it appears to be scarily calorific – tweak it, as suggested, and the calories will come tumbling down. Better still, don't worry. Remember, eating exactly this food caused me to lose 4 stone.

Your Diet Not Mine

Muddled crab and oyster sauce + fragrant rice (page 30)
325 kcals/1358 kjoules
Pot-roast chicken + cabbage, morels and squash (page 31)
384 kcals/1622 kjoules
Pot-luck veg (page 32) *320 kcals/1324 kjoules*

Working Woman's Reality

Warm mushroom and prawn salad (page 38)
220 kcals/909 kjoules
Jazzed-up scrambled eggs on mushrooms (page 39)
370 kcals/1540 kjoules
Smoked fish + Japanese rice (page 40)
494 kcals/2068 kjoules
Mrs Klein's tuna fish salad (page 42)
444 kcals/1870 kjoules
Chilled Japanese noodles (page 43)
495 kcals/2099 kjoules
Springtime scrambled eggs (page 44)
311 kcals/1292 kjoules
Omelettes (page 45) *340 kcals/1423 kjoules*
Hijiki (page 46) *70 kcals/285 kjoules*
Baked potato + nice stuffings (page 49):
  Coriander and pistachio raita *400 kcals/1571 kjoules*;
  Bacon and avocado mayo *536 kcals/2267 kjoules*
Aubergine dip + crudités (page 50)
356k cals/1473 kjoules
Hard-boiled eggs + dukkah (page 51)
35 kcals/148 kjoules per egg

The packet queen

Spruced-up vegetable soup (page 53)
320 kcals/1361 kjoules
Caesar salad + peas and prawns (page 54)
350 kcals/1479 kjoules
Instant ramen or miso soup + extra bits (page 56):
  Ramen soup *441 kcals/1843 kjoules*;
  Miso soup *85 kcals/356 kjoules*
Air-cured ham + fresh figs (page 57)
115 kcals/483 kjoules
Gravlax + guacamole (page 59) *160 kcals/669 kjoules*
Warm chicken tikka + tzatziki salad (page 60)
150 kcals/620 kjoules

Nice easy things to do with a bag of salad (page 61):
  Mixed leaves *370 kcals/1533 kjoules*;
  Wild rocket *322 kcals/1383 kjoules*;
  Watercress *441 kcals/1874 kjoules*;
  Little gem *490 kcals/2042 kjoules*;
  Ruby chard and beetroot *345kcals/1430 kjoules*

Eating With Your Darling

Smoked haddock + poached egg (page 66)
230 kcals/977 kjoules
Aubergine 'lasagne' (page 68) *320 kcals/1338 kjoules*
Griddled scallops + tomato and ginger sauce (page 69)
370 kcals/1544 kjoules
Grilled sardines + lemon and garlic couscous stuffing
  (page 70) *380 kcals/1583 kjoules*
Salmon teriyaki + wilted greens (page 72)
480 kcals/1996 kjoules
Spice-rubbed cod + vegetables (page 75)
290 kcals/1217 kjoules
Warm chicken liver and grape salad (page 76)
292 kcals/1222 kjoules
Calves' liver + sweet and sour courgettes (page 77)
270 kcals/1111 kjoules
Yoghurt-marinated chicken + spiced green lentils
  (page 78) *490 kcals/2074 kjoules*
Lindsey B's warm chicken and runner bean salad
  (page 81) *322 kcals/1345 kjoules*
The best lamb burgers (page 82) *465 kcals/1935 kjoules*
One-pan pork and peppers (page 84)
271 kcals/1133 kjoules
Lamb chops + garlic and spinach pilaf (page 85)
695 kcals/2905 kjoules
Tofu, shiitake and coriander broth (page 87)
360 kcals/1528 kjoules
Green onion soup (page 88) *300 kcals/1250 kjoules*
Spinach, broad bean and artichoke salad (page 89)
226 kcals/1013 kjoules

Big Food Recipes

Squash, bean and onion soup (page 103)
186 kcals/790 kjoules
Minestrone soup (page 104) *156 kcals/657 kjoules*
Tofu rice and pak choi broth (page 105)
250 kcals/1058 kjoules
Mushroom broth + prawn and pork wontons (page 106)
300 kcals/1260 kjoules
Prawn laksa (page 108) *548 kcals/2309 kjoules*
Chilli squid + ribbon veg salad (page 110)
268 kcals/1128 kjoules
Thai-style mussels (page 113) *215 kcals/917 kjoules*
One-pan chicken, sugar snaps and tamarind (page 114)
345 kcals/1441 kjoules
Gingered pork and scallops (page 115)
480 kcals/2028 kjoules
Chicken, shiitake and miso broth (page 116)
300 kcals/1268 kjoules

Slow Food Recipes

An asparagus feast + soft-boiled eggs (page 118)
300 kcals/1262 kjoules
Roast quail + 5-spice marinade (page 120)
250 kcals/1036 kjoules

Chinese-style chicken wings (page 123)
470 kcals/1959 kjoules
Lebanese chicken wings (page 124)
310 kcals/1290 kjoules
Skinny lamb chops + herb paste (page 125)
326 kcals/1369 kjoules
Fiddly prawn and chilli salad (page 126)
104 kcals/434 kjoules
Cold lobster + coriander dipping sauce (page 128)
200 kcals/840 kjoules

Beyond Baked Beans

A Bigger Splash (page 138):
  Nearly Virgin Mary *41 kcals/179 kjoules*;
  Spritz *160 kcals/665 kjoules*;
  Bellini *80 kcals/335 kjoules*;
  Bucks fizz *83 kcals/350 kjoules*

Starters

Cantaloupe and crab salad + ginger dressing (page 140)
229 kcals/955 kjoules
Asian-spiced prawns (page 142) *110 kcals/453 kjoules*
Smoked eel, cucumber and radish salad (page 143)
75 kcals/305 kjoules
Vietnamese rice paper rolls (page 145)
250 kcals/1057 kjoules
Seared beef carpaccio + mustard sauce (page 146)
222 kcals/927 kjoules
Jambon persillé (page 148) *327 kcals/1370 kjoules*
Grilled red pepper and chicory salad + shaved Parmesan
  (page 150) *135 kcals/560 kjoules*
Griddled leek and feta salad (page 153)
310 kcals/1272 kjoules
Smoked ham + Thai melon salad (page 154)
142 kcals/600 kjoules
Buffalo mozzarella + Comice pears (page 155)
290 kcals/1230 kjoules

Main courses

Ruddy fish stew (page 156) *300 kcals/1263 kjoules*
Seared scallops + black tagliolini (page 159)
485 kcals/2054 kjoules
Baked hake + wheatgrain and roast vegetable hash
  (page 160) *378 kcals/1596 kjoules*
Seared cod with green olive crust (page 161)
219 kcals/922 kjoules
Rare beef salad + lime and chilli dressing (page 162)
350 kcals/1470 kjoules
One-pan Chinese chicken (page 163)
263 kcals/1101 kjoules
Braised loin of pork + oregano and fennel (page 164)
450 kcals/1900 kjoules

Puddings

Sparkling Muscat (or other fruit) jelly (page 167)
171 kcals/722 kjoules
Rosy fruit terrine (page 168) *160 kcals/670 kjoules*
Mango and lime granita (page 169) *380 kcals/1623 kjoules*
Winter fruit salad (page 172) *80 kcals/342 kjoules*
Spiced fruit compote (page 173) *255 kcals/1068 kjoules*
French apple tarts (page 174) *270 kcals/1174 kjoules*

Sod It

Hot bitter chocolate mousse + thick Jersey cream
  (page 188) *469 kcals/1958 kjoules*